Fat Quarter
FRENZY

Susan Purney-Mark

Daphne Greig

American Quilter's Society

P. O. Box 3290 • Paducah, KY 42002-3290

www.AQSquilt.com

Located in Paducah, Kentucky, the American Quilter's Society (AQS) is dedicated to promoting the accomplishments of today's quilters. Through its publications and events, AQS strives to honor today's quiltmakers and their work and to inspire future creativity and innovation in quiltmaking.

EDITOR: TRACEY JOHNSON
COPY EDITOR: CHRYSTAL ABHALTER
GRAPHIC DESIGN: AMY CHASE
COVER DESIGN: MICHAEL BUCKINGHAM
QUILT PHOTOS: CHARLES R. LYNCH

Library of Congress Cataloging-in-Publication Data

Purney-Mark, Susan.
   Fat quarter frenzy / by Susan Purney-Mark and Daphne Greig.
       p. cm.
   Summary: "Quiltmaking projects using fat quarters. Includes a teachers' guide section for developing classes"--Provided by publisher.
   ISBN 1-57432-870-0
   1. Patchwork--Patterns. 2. Quilting.   I. Greig, Daphne. II. Title.

TT835.P8697 2005
746.46'041--dc22

                                    2004028327

Additional copies of this book may be ordered from the American Quilter's Society, PO Box 3290, Paducah, KY 42002-3290, or call 1-800-626-5420 or online at www.AmericanQuilter.com.

Acknowledgments

Quilting has been our passion for many years, and we have been fortunate in creating and building a business with our publishing, teaching, writing, and lecturing. Along the way, we have made many friendships. These people have been the foundation of the development and creation of this book, and we value their input and guidance.

For our friends who tested our designs and read the directions, we thank Mary Lou Arnsdorf, Rose Bates, Darlene Dressler, Peggy Farries, Wenche Hemphill, Shelley Polkinghorne, and Carol Turnham.

Thanks to Starr Designs Hand Dyed Fabric for providing the fabric for MOON RINGS.

We also thank our friends at the American Quilter's Society, who have shown faith in us as quilters and writers. Special thanks go to Barbara Smith and Tracey Johnson.

We treasure our families for their unwavering support, encouragement, and cooking! Special thanks go to our husbands, Alan and Henry.

Table of Contents

Fig. 1–1. Fat quarters can be attractively packaged by shops.

General Instructions

What's a Fat Quarter?

A fat quarter is a quarter yard of fabric cut in an unusual way. A regular quarter yard is a strip 9" by the full width (about 44"–45") of the fabric. This isn't a lot of fabric, but it can be useful for many projects.

However, what if you needed to cut a 10" square for your project? Your quarter yard would not work. So, quilt shops have developed a way to provide the same amount of fabric, but it's cut in a shape that is more useful for quilters. They cut a half-yard of fabric (about 18" x 44½") into two pieces, each measuring about 18" x 22¼". This cut is made along the fabric fold and yields two fat quarters.

Now you can cut that 10" square for your project from one of the fat quarters. You can actually cut two 10" squares from one fat quarter.

While all of the projects presented are cut from fat quarters, we have taken into account that fabric may shrink when washed. Our measurements, therefore, are based on a fat quarter size of 17" x 20½". The diagrams in the projects will show you how to cut your fat quarters for that project.

Shopping for Fat Quarters

Fat quarters are fun to buy, give, and trade. They're like a box of chocolates ... it's hard to stop at just one! They're portable, and a couple of fat quarters can slip into an envelope for mailing. They'll bring a smile to a special friend, and they're great to trade and use for prizes. They are also great souvenirs to purchase while you are traveling or visiting quilt shows.

Quilters often buy fat quarters when they find a wonderful fabric and want just a small sample. Buying in this way helps to build a good inventory.

Some quilters concentrate on collecting a particular type of fabric, such as Japanese-style prints, blue-and-white fabrics, or polka-dots. When a quilter has enough in her collection, it's quiltmaking time. Then she can begin collecting something else.

Many shops package groups of fat quarters together (fig. 1–1). The fat quarters may be from one line of fabric by a manufacturer or they may have some common element, such landscape scenes, floral prints, or primary colors. Many shops also have unique ways to package their fat quarters, making them even more enticing. We'll find them beautifully displayed in shops and catalogs or on the Internet, ready for us to purchase and cheerfully bring home.

Selecting Fabrics

There are a lot of different ways to choose your fat quarters. Most of our projects suggest fabric selection based on value: light, medium, or dark. We offer you a range of quilts that vary in size, color, technique, and design. We're sure you will find many ideas to entice you to pull out your stash of fat quarters and play.

Remember to look closely at your stash. Search for color, value, or print groups that are sparse or missing. Fat quarters provide a great way to build up inventory. Arrange with one or several friends to buy half-yard fabric pieces then cut them in half to share with one another.

Fat quarter quilts are not necessarily scrap quilts. They can have a planned color or value scheme with a variety of print designs. In fact, variety within a range will offer more visual interest than will staying within a more limited range.

Substituting Yardage

One of the best things about fat quarters is the endless variety they offer us. There are so many fabrics to choose from. If you would rather use yardage, add up the number of fat quarters for each color or value and divide by four. (Four fat quarters equal one yard.) So if the project requires four light fat quarters, you will need one yard of light fabric. If the project requires seven medium fat quarters, you will need 1¾ yards of a medium fabric.

In some of our designs, you can substitute scraps for fat quarters. Read each step in the project and measure carefully if you wish to make any substitutions.

Caring for Fabrics

We recommend prewashing your fabrics before using them in your quilt projects. However, the agitation and tumbling in a washing machine can tangle fabrics the size of a fat quarter, so we recommend this method:

1. Fill your sink with lukewarm water and a gentle soap.

2. Add your fat quarters, divided by color, and wet them thoroughly. Begin with the lightest colors, remove them, then add the next darkest colors until all the groups have been soaked. Squeeze out the excess water as you remove each group of fat quarters.

3. Now, drain the wash water. Refill the sink with lukewarm water and rinse the groups of fat quarters until no soap remains. Change the rinse water as needed until all the groups have been rinsed. Roll the groups of fat quarters in a towel to remove excess water, then place the fat quarters in your dryer on a low heat setting.

4. Remove the fat quarters when they are damp-dry and press with an iron. Be sure the fabrics are completely dry before folding them for storage.

Get into the habit of prewashing your fabrics as soon as you bring them home so they go into your storage area all ready to be used.

Storing Fat Quarters

There are as many ways to store fabrics as there are quilters. Some quilters prefer to arrange their fabrics by color, while others arrange their fabrics by type (floral, geometric, solids, etc.). Still others arrange their fat quarters separately from other yardage. Whatever sorting method you choose, you will want the fabric accessible when you need it. You don't want the frustration of searching for that fabric you know you have but can't find.

Plastic containers or wire baskets can keep fabrics sorted. They also can be stacked to save storage space. If you have shelves on which to store your folded fabrics,

you may find arranging fabrics on end convenient, because you can see fairly quickly what is available in your fabric "pantry" (fig. 1–2, fig. 1–2a).

Having Fun with Fat Quarters

Quilters are sharing people. We love to show off our latest purchases, share our favorite places to shop, and have fun exchanging fabrics. Some quilters and groups even make games that involve fat quarter exchanges.

Here are some ideas you might like to try with your friends:

Surprise exchange. Each person brings a fat quarter she doesn't think she will ever use and places it in a paper bag. (All of the fabrics that are brought should be good-quality, 100 percent cotton. It's fun to see what prints will show up.) Each person selects a new paper bag. Many times the recipient of what someone else no longer wants is grateful for the fat quarter won. One quilter's ugly fat quarter may be another quilter's fabulous find.

Fat quarter birthday gift event. Decorate a cardboard box to look like a cake. Put holes in the top of the box. Roll up donated fat quarters and put them in the holes, with a paper "flame" in the top of each fat quarter. While the group sings "Happy Birth-

Fig. 1–2. A method of storing fat quarters

Fig. 1–2a. Another method of storing fat quarters

day," each member who has a birthday that month selects a fat quarter gift.

Matching fat quarters game. This is a good way for guild members to meet one another and mingle. Invite each guild member to bring two identical fat quarters to a meeting. Each member keeps one fat quarter and puts the matching one in a basket or bag. Then, each member pulls a new fat quarter out of the bag and searches for the member who has the matching fabric. Members go home with one of their original fat quarters, a new fat quarter, and perhaps a new friend.

Monthly fat quarter draw. Some online groups have a monthly fat quarter draw. Quilters mail a fat quarter and a postage stamp to the organizer each month. Each person's name goes into the draw once for each fat quarter sent in. One winner's name is drawn at the end of the month and the stamps are used to mail all the fat quarters to the winner. Then, the winner posts a picture of the packet he or she has won.

Gift basket. For a special friend in need of a pick-me-up, purchase a quilt book with a theme. Ask each member of the guild to contribute one fat quarter that relates to the theme to make a special gift basket.

Tools and Supplies

These are the basic tools and supplies you will need to make the projects. Several offer technique options; for example, hand appliqué or machine appliqué. Select the method you like best.

 **Rotary cutter.** Select a cutter that feels comfortable in your hand. Be sure to change the blade frequently, because a sharp blade will help you make accurate cuts.

 Rotary-cutting mat. Your rotary cutting mat should be large enough for a piece of fabric folded once selvage to selvage. You may want a smaller mat for special techniques, such as cutting around templates.

Rulers. You will need a 6" x 24" ruler with the 1/8" increments clearly marked. Smaller rulers will also be helpful; for example, a 6" square ruler is useful for cutting units from strips of fabric. A large square ruler (12" or more) is useful for squaring up your blocks.

 **Scissors.** A pair of sharp fabric scissors and a pair of small embroidery scissors are useful for cutting fabric and snipping threads.

 Sewing machine. A basic well-tuned sewing machine will be needed. If you have or can purchase a 1/4" patchwork foot, it will be invaluable for sewing accurate seams. Built-in stitches, such as a zigzag, buttonhole or blind-hem, are useful for machine appliqué. Your machine will function best if it has a sharp needle. For general purposes, we use a jeans/denim, 80/12 needle.

 Thread. You will need 100 percent cotton thread for machine piecing. We use light and dark neutral colors, such as gray, beige, and tan. Use dark thread only when your fabrics are very dark. Use a lightweight cotton thread for machine appliqué. You can also use decorative threads (rayon or polyester) for machine appliqué. We like to use lightweight cotton or silk thread for hand appliqué. For quilting, use hand-quilting thread when stitching by hand and use invisible nylon thread, cotton, or decorative threads for machine quilting.

Hand-sewing needles. You will need appliqué needles for hand appliqué and quilting betweens for hand quilting. You may also like to use a thimble for hand sewing.

Pins. Use fine, sharp straight pins to accurately match seams. We like the ones with glass heads because they are easier to see and handle. For pin basting your quilt layers, use non-rusting safety pins designed for quilters. These can be curved or straight.

 **Fabric markers.** You will need to mark sewing lines in some of the projects. Choose a marker that makes a fine line. You may need two markers: a light marker for dark fabric and a dark marker for light fabric. You may also need to mark lines for quilting. Test the markers on fabric scraps to be sure the marks can be removed.

 Iron and ironing board. A clean steam iron and large ironing surface will give you the best results. Be sure to press carefully as you complete each step in your project.

Template plastic. Templates can be made with any sturdy material. Heavy cardboard is one choice, but it is easier to use plastic that is designed for templates. You can see through the plastic to accurately trace the template patterns and to transfer any markings, such as piece number and grain line. The plastic can be easily cut with scissors or a rotary cutter and ruler. Be sure to check that your templates are accurate before cutting fabric for your project.

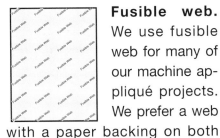 **Fusible web.** We use fusible web for many of our machine appliqué projects. We prefer a web with a paper backing on both sides. We recommend using an appliqué pressing sheet to keep your iron and ironing board clean. Follow the manufacturer's directions for your chosen product, including the iron temperature and fusing time.

 **Batting.** Your batting choice depends on the size of the project, whether you are going to quilt by hand or by machine, and how you are going to use the quilt. Polyester battings are lighter in weight, generally have a higher loft, and are easy to quilt.

Cotton and cotton-blend battings are firmer, have a lovely drape, and may be a little more difficult to hand quilt. Our batting of choice is an 80 percent cotton and 20 percent polyester blend which is easy to hand or machine quilt, has a good weight for both wallhangings and bed quilts, and is simple to clean.

Fat Quarter Projects
Four Patch Harmony

Quilt Size: 56" x 72"

FOUR-PATCH HARMONY, by Susan Purney-Mark

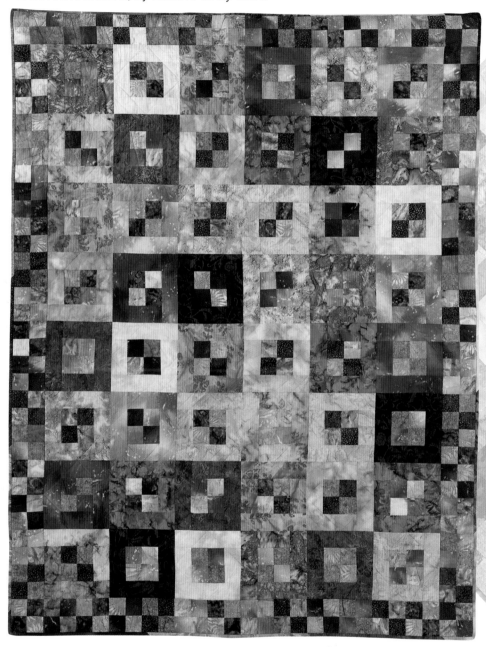

This is a simple quilt with a lot of impact. It is easy to make, and it would be perfect made in batiks, such as we've used. The collections of new fabrics from manufacturers would work well as would a color-based selection of bright fabrics from your stash. There's a lot of opportunity to have fun here!

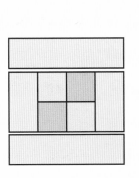

Shopping List

Amount of Fabric

21 fat quarters, from lights to darks
for blocks & borders
Leftover strips from fat quarters for binding
3 ½ yards for backing
60" x 76" piece of batting

Cutting Instructions

Before cutting, divide your fat quarters into one group of nine and one group of 12. Place a balance of light, medium, and dark colors in each group.

■ Group 1

From each of the nine fat quarters, cut 48 squares that are 2½" x 2½" (fig. 2–1). You will have a total of 432 squares for the blocks and borders.

■ Group 2

From each of the 12 fat quarters, cut eight rectangles 2½" x 8½" and eight rectangles 2½" x 4½" (fig. 2–2). You need 96 rectangles of both sizes for the center blocks.

■ Binding

With scraps from the fat quarters, cut 15 strips 2"–2¼" x 20½", depending on the width of your fat quarters.

Sewing the Quilt

1. Sort the 2½" squares into sets containing four squares each (two squares from each of two different fabrics). Sew two different squares together to make a pair. Join two pairs to make each four-patch unit. Make 108 units measuring 4½".

2. Using two long and two short rectangles of the same fabric for each block, sew rectangles to the edges of each four-patch unit to complete a block. (fig. 2–3). Make 48 blocks.

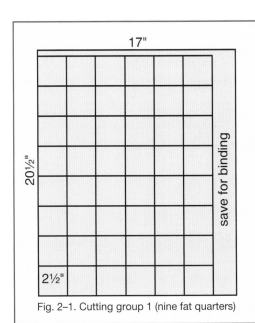

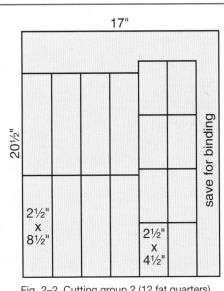

Fig. 2–1. Cutting group 1 (nine fat quarters)	Fig. 2–2. Cutting group 2 (12 fat quarters)	Fig. 2–3. Block assembly

17"
20½"
save for binding
2½"

17"
20½"
save for binding
2½" x 8½"
2½" x 4½"

3. Arrange the blocks, moving them around until you are satisfied with the placement. Rotate the blocks so that every other block has the longer rectangles on the top and bottom. Sew the blocks into rows then sew the rows together.

4. Make the border by arranging the remaining four-patch units into two rows of 16 and two rows of 14 with a pleasing color arrangement. Sew the units into border strips. Sew the long borders to the sides of the quilt, then sew the shorter borders to the top and the bottom of the quilt (fig. 2–4).

5. Mark your quilting design on the quilt. We quilted a diagonal square, then worked a simple line toward the center of each block. The border was quilted in an easy Greek key design.

6. Layer the quilt with backing and batting and quilt by hand or machine. Use your favorite method and use the 2"–2¼" leftover strips to bind your quilt. Depending on the width of your binding strips, make single-fold or double-fold binding.

Fig. 2–4. Quilt assembly

Lolly Hearts
Table Topper

Quilt size 29" x 29"
LOLLY HEARTS TABLE TOPPER, by Susan Purney-Mark

This cute little table topper makes up quickly as a special gift or centerpiece for a party. Use fusible web or your favorite product for the appliqué and a lightweight batting to help it drape nicely over a table.

Shopping List

Amount of Fabric

2 different fat quarters for background squares
& outer border
2 different fat quarters for four-patch units
1 fat quarter for small & large hearts (pink)
1 fat quarter for large hearts, leaves, stems
& cornerstones (green)
2 fat quarters for inner border, binding & cornerstones
1 yard for fusible web (optional)
35" square for backing
35" square of low-loft batting

Cutting Instructions

■ **Background (for hearts)**
From one fat quarter, cut nine squares 5½" (fig. 2–5).

■ **Background**
(for squares and outer border)
From one fat quarter, cut four squares 5½" for background blocks and seven strips 1½" for the outer border (fig. 2–6).

■ **Four-patch units**
Layer the two fat quarters, right sides together, and cut through both layers to make 24 squares 3" (fig. 2–7.) You will have a total of 48 squares, 24 of each color.

■ **Hearts, leaves & stems**
For machine appliqué, trace the appliqué patterns on pages 18–19 onto fusible web. Use the web manufacturer's instructions to fuse the web shapes.

From the pink fat quarter, fuse four large hearts, four small hearts, and one center circle. From the green fat quarter, fuse and cut four large hearts, eight leaves, and four stems. Cut each fused shape on the line. (For hand appliqué, add a turn-under allowance by eye when cutting the fabric pieces. Omit the fusible web.)

■ **Inner border & binding**
From one of the fat quarters, cut

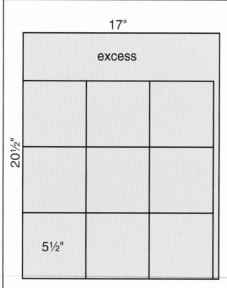

Fig. 2–5. Cutting for heart background (one fat quarter)

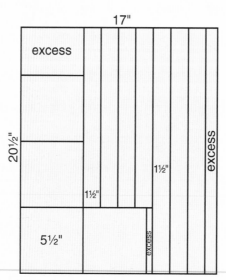

Fig. 2–6. Cutting for squares and outer border (one fat quarter)

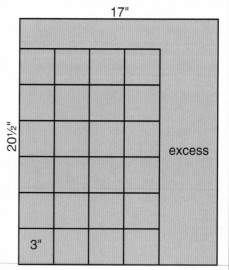

Fig. 2–7. Cutting for four-patch units (two different fat quarters)

six strips 1½" x 20½" for the inner border. From the other fat quarter, cut seven strips 1½" for binding.

■ Cornerstones

From the green remainders, cut four squares 1½" for the inner border cornerstones. From the inner border remainders, cut four squares 1½" for the outer border cornerstones.

Sewing the Table Topper

1. Referring to the block assembly diagram (fig. 2–8), sew the four-patch units. Make 12. The units should measure 5½" square.

2. Referring to the quilt assembly diagram (fig. 2–9), arrange the four-patch units with the 5½" squares to form the body of the quilt. Sew the units and squares into rows then join the rows.

3. Join the six inner border strips, with diagonal seams, to form one long strip. Cut four 25½" lengths from the strip. Sew the side inner borders to the quilt top. Add the green cornerstones to the remaining two border strips. Sew those strips to the top and bottom of the quilt top.

4. Join the outer border strips into one long strip. Cut the strip into four 27½" lengths. Sew two strips to the sides of the quilt. Sew the cornerstones cut from the inner border fabric to the remaining strips and sew them to the top and bottom of the quilt.

5. Referring to the photo on page 15, arrange the appliqué shapes on the quilt top. Tuck the stem ends under the hearts and center circle. Place the leaf ends on top of the stems. Following the fusing directions for your product, fuse the shapes in place.

6. Stitch the edges of the appliqué shapes, matching the thread color to the appliqué shapes and choosing your desired appliqué stitch. Check to see the variety of stitches that your machine can do.

7. Mark your quilting design on the table topper. We used a diagonal cross-hatching design and quilted around each appliqué shape. The borders were quilted in the ditch.

8. Layer the table topper with backing and batting and quilt by hand or by machine. Use the 1½" strips (sewn end to end with diagonal seams) to bind the table topper.

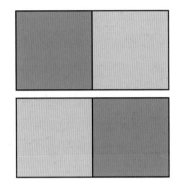

Fig. 2–8. Make 12 four-patch units.

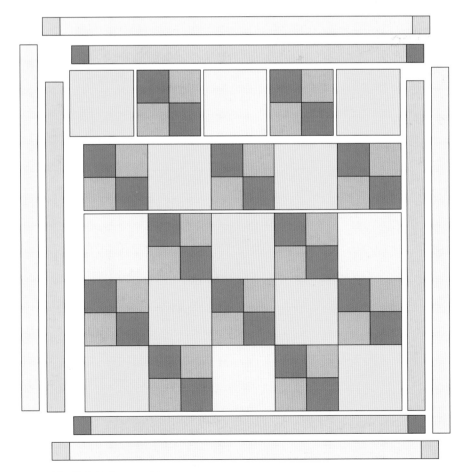

Fig. 2–9. Quilt assembly

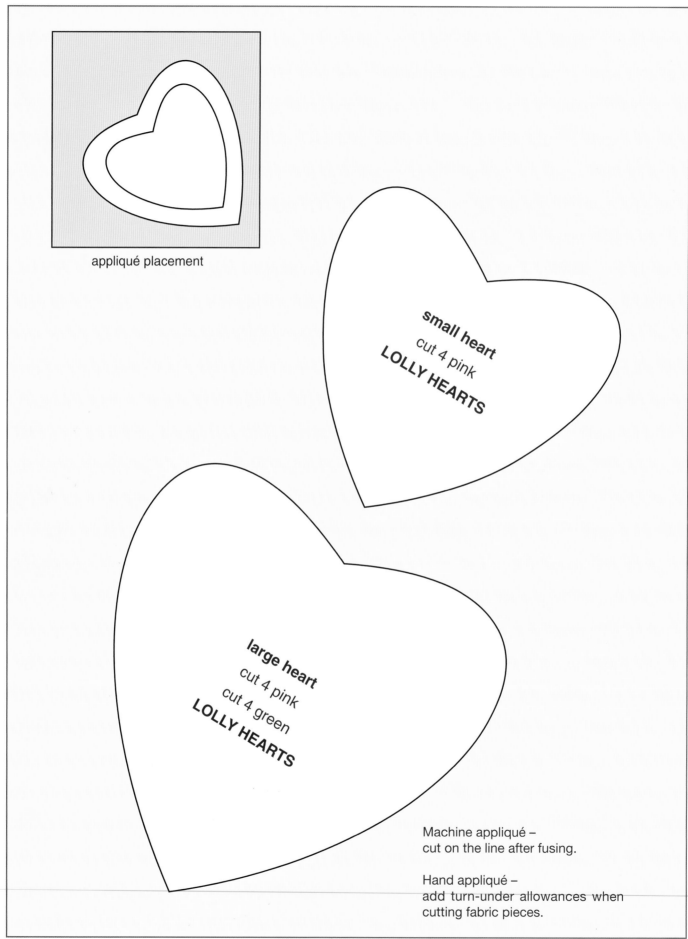

appliqué placement

small heart
cut 4 pink
LOLLY HEARTS

large heart
cut 4 pink
cut 4 green
LOLLY HEARTS

Machine appliqué –
cut on the line after fusing.

Hand appliqué –
add turn-under allowances when
cutting fabric pieces.

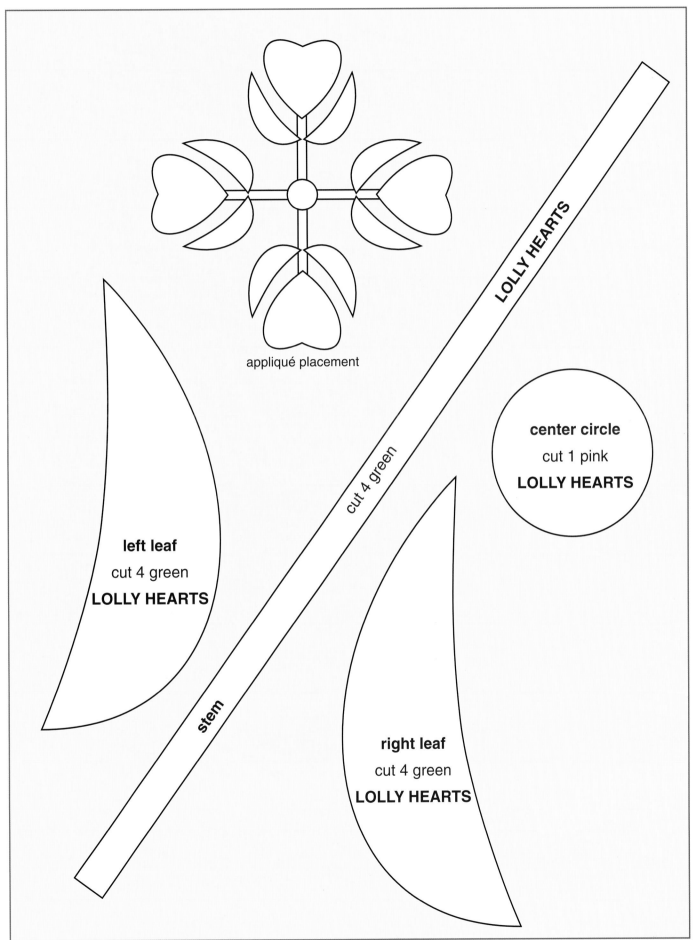

appliqué placement

LOLLY HEARTS

cut 4 green

center circle
cut 1 pink
LOLLY HEARTS

left leaf
cut 4 green
LOLLY HEARTS

stem

right leaf
cut 4 green
LOLLY HEARTS

Moon Rings

Quilt size 51" x 51"
MOON RINGS, by Daphne Greig

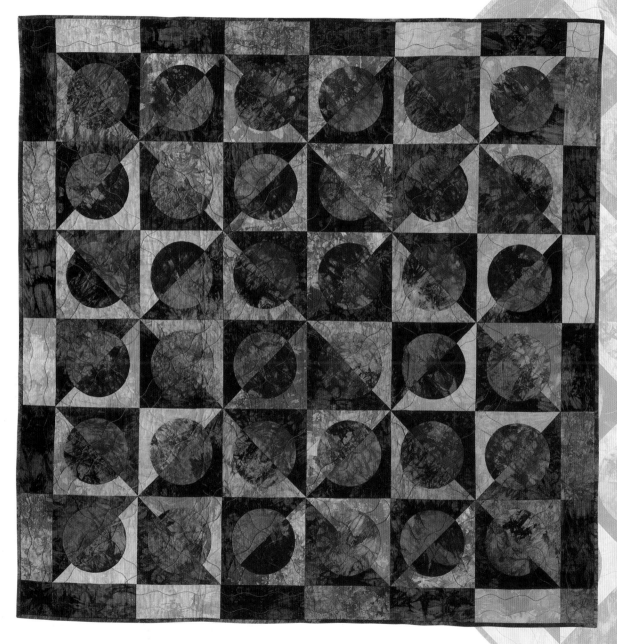

Practice your appliqué skills with this quilt. We appliquéd the
circles by hand, but you can use your favorite method. We
selected some lovely hand-dyed fabrics for our quilt. This
design would be equally nice in tone-on-tone fabrics or even
shades of black, white, and gray. Pay close attention to
value when you choose your fabrics.

See the Moon Rings Bonus Project, page 24, for an additional quilt you can make from the appliqué cutouts left over from the wall quilt.

Cutting Instructions

■ **Block backgrounds**
Match light and dark fat quarters in pairs, right sides together. Repeat for pairs of medium light and very dark fat quarters. You will have six pairs, three of each combination.

From two of the light/dark and two of the medium light/very dark pairs, cut four squares 8½" (fig. 2–10). You will have 16 pairs of squares, eight in each value combination. Keep the pairs of squares layered together.

From the third pair of fat quarters in each value combination, cut one square 8½" (fig. 2–11). Keep the squares layered together. You

Shopping List

Amount of Fabric

Light — 3 different fat quarters for blocks & border
Medium light — 3 different fat quarters for blocks & border
Dark — 3 different fat quarters for blocks & border
Very dark — 3 different fat quarters for blocks & border
Medium — 8 different fat quarters for circles & binding
3 yards of fusible web (optional)
3¼ yards for backing
54" square of batting

will have a total of 18 pairs of squares, nine pairs in each value combination. Set aside the layered remainders for borders.

■ **Circles**
Select four pairs of medium fat quarters that you would like to use for the circles. Place the

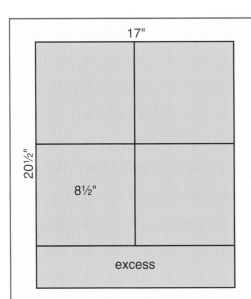

Fig. 2–10. Cutting for block backgrounds (two light/dark pairs and two medium light/very dark pairs of fat quarters)

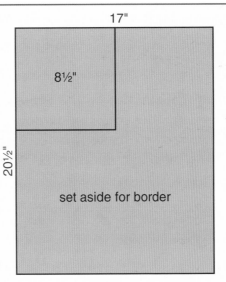

Fig. 2–11. Cutting for one pair of light/dark and one pair of medium light/very dark fat quarters

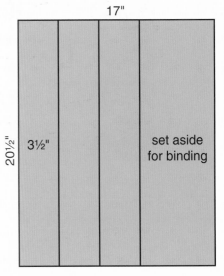

Fig. 2–12. Cutting for medium fabric strips to make circles (four pairs of fat quarters)

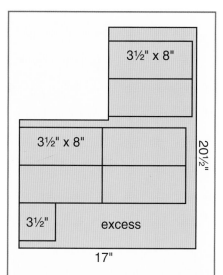

3½" x 8"

3½" x 8"

3½"   excess

20½"

17"

Fig. 2–13. Cutting for remainders of light/dark and medium light/very dark fabrics for borders and cornerstones

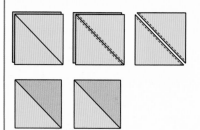

Fig. 2–14. Make 36 half-square triangle units for the background blocks.

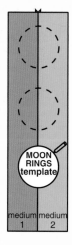

MOON RINGS template

medium 1 medium 2

Fig. 2–15. Trace the circle template on fabric strip pairs. Trace and cut out 36.

Fig. 2–16. Block assembly

pairs right sides together. From each pair, cut three strips 3½" x 20½" (fig. 2–12, page 21). You will have 12 pairs of strips. Keep the pairs of strips layered together. Set aside the remainders for binding.

■ Borders & cornerstones
Use the remainders from the light/dark and medium light/very dark fat quarters to cut the border strips. From each fabric, cut six rectangles 3½" x 8" and one square 3½" (fig. 2–13). You will have a total of 24 rectangles and four squares.

■ Binding
Use six of the medium fat quarter remainders for binding. From each fabric, cut two strips 2¼" x 20½". You will have a total of 12 strips.

Sewing the Wall Quilt

1. For the block backgrounds, make half-square triangle units with the layered 8½" squares, as follows: Draw a diagonal line, corner to corner, on the wrong side of the light and very light squares. Sew ¼" on each side of the line. Cut on the line and press the seam allowances toward the darker fabric. Trim the sewn squares to 8" (fig. 2–14). You will have 36 half-square triangle units: 18 light/dark and 18 medium light/very dark.

2. Make circles by sewing the pairs of 3½" medium strips together along their long edges.

Press the seam allowances open. Using the circle template on page 25, trace three circles on each pair of strips, by aligning the center line on the template with the strip's seam (fig. 2–15). For hand appliqué, add turn-under allowance by eye. For machine appliqué, trace 36 circles onto the paper side of fusible web, leaving about ½" between circles. Cut apart, leaving about ¼" around each circle. Fuse three circles to the wrong side of each pair of strips, aligning the center line on the paper circle with the strip's seam. Cut 36 circles.

3. Pair the circles and background blocks so they have a strong contrast in value. Position the circles on the squares, aligning the seam lines, and use your favorite method to appliqué them in place (fig. 2–16). You will have 36 blocks.

4. Arrange the blocks in six rows, with six blocks in each row. See the quilt photo as a guide for arranging the blocks. There are many other quilt layout options (fig. 2–17). Sew the blocks together in rows and then sew the rows together. Press all the seams open for a flatter quilt top.

5. Make the borders by arranging the 3½" x 8" rectangles into four strips, each containing six rectangles. Sew the rectangles together end to end to make four border strips. Press the seam allowances open.

6. Sew the side borders to the quilt. Add one 3½" cornerstone square to each end of the remaining two border strips. Sew these border strips to the top and the bottom of the quilt (fig. 2–18).

7. Mark the quilting design on the quilt top. We machine quilted a double wavy line placed diagonally across the quilt and around the border.

8. Layer the quilt top with backing and batting. Quilt by hand or by machine. Make the binding by sewing the 2¼" medium fabric strips in one continuous strip. Use your favorite method to bind the quilt.

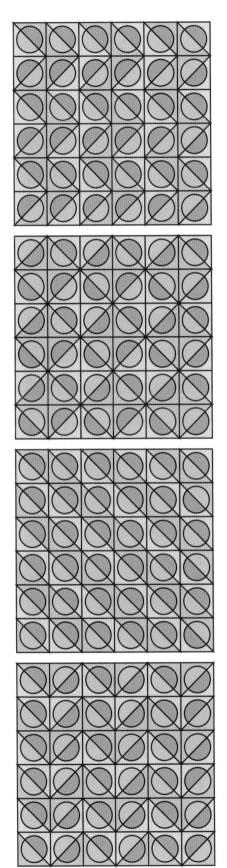

Fig. 2–17. Layout options

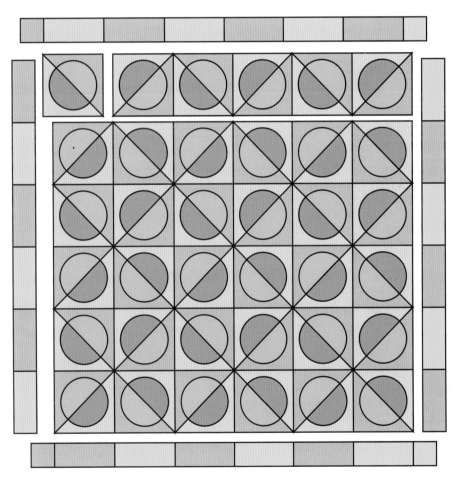

Fig. 2–18. Quilt assembly diagram

Moon Rings Bonus Project

As mentioned, we used hand appliqué for our MOON RINGS quilt. We like to cut away the background fabric behind the appliqué shapes when we use this method. When we did this, we had large pieces of fabric that were much too good to waste.

We carefully cut the excess fabric circles of background behind the appliquéd circles and then trimmed the pieces to make 36 half-square triangle units 3½" square. When trimming, we were careful to keep the diagonal seam exactly on the diagonal of the squares.

We arranged the squares in six rows, each containing six squares. Just as with the larger quilt, there are several different color arrangement options for these squares.

We layered our small quilt with backing and batting and used some of our decorative machine stitches for the quilting.

We cut strips 1½" wide from remaining pieces of the fat quarters to bind our small quilt.

MOON RINGS Bonus Project, 18" x 18", by Daphne Greig

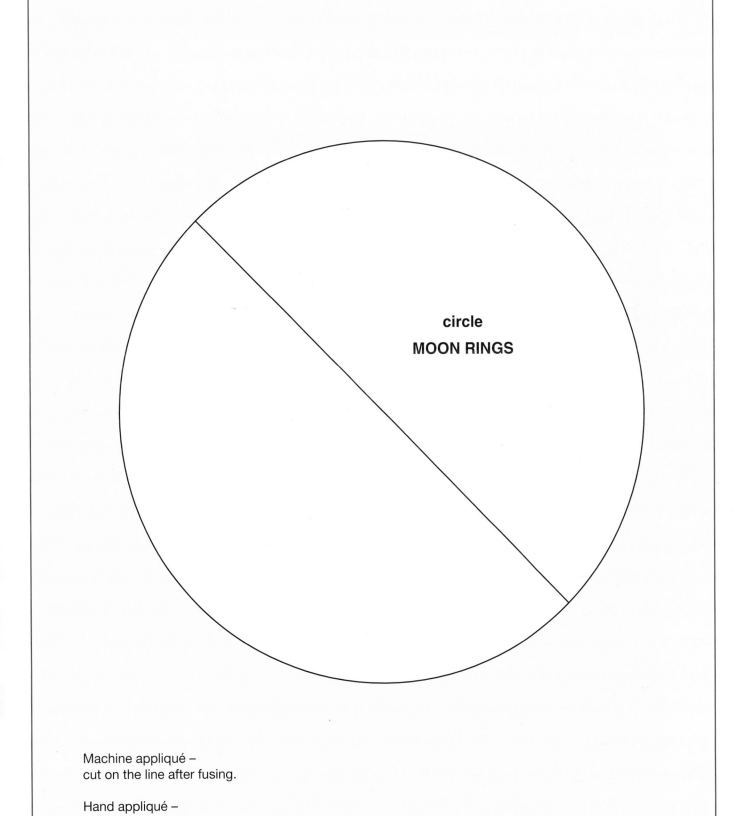

circle
MOON RINGS

Machine appliqué –
cut on the line after fusing.

Hand appliqué –
add turn-under allowances when cutting
fabric pieces.

Bamboo Grove

Quilt size 38" x 50½"
BAMBOO GROVE, by Daphne Greig

Rows of leafy strips are combined for this wall quilt. Try the rich colors of a bamboo forest or bright, sunny fabrics for a fresh look. The bamboo theme is continued in the BAMBOO GROVE TABLE RUNNER on page 29.

Shopping List

Amount of Fabric

6 different fat quarters for background
5 different fat quarters for leaves
1⅞ yards for vertical strips, border & binding
2½ yards of fusible web (optional)
1½ yards for backing
42" x 54" piece of batting

First, cut five strips 2¼" across the fabric for binding.

From the remaining fabric, which should measure at least 51¾" x 42", cut the following strips lengthwise: three strips 1½" (between rows of leaves), two strips 2½" (between pairs of leaf rows), and four strips 4½" (borders).

Sewing the Wall Quilt

1. Use template plastic or cardboard to make a leaf template from the pattern on page 32. For machine appliqué, trace the template onto the paper side of the fusible web 66 times, leaving about ½" between each leaf. Cut apart, leaving about ¼" around each leaf.

2. Sew two different 1¾" x 17" leaf strips together on their long edges (fig. 2–21, page 28). Press the seam allowances open. Repeat with the remaining leaf

Cutting Instructions

■ Background blocks
From each of five fat quarters, cut 12 squares 4½". From one fat quarter, cut six squares 4½" (fig. 2–19). You will have a total of 66 squares.

■ Strips for leaves
From each of five fat quarters, cut nine strips 1¾" x 17" (fig. 2–20). You will have a total of 45 strips. You will use 44 strips for the quilt and have one extra.

■ Vertical strips, border & binding

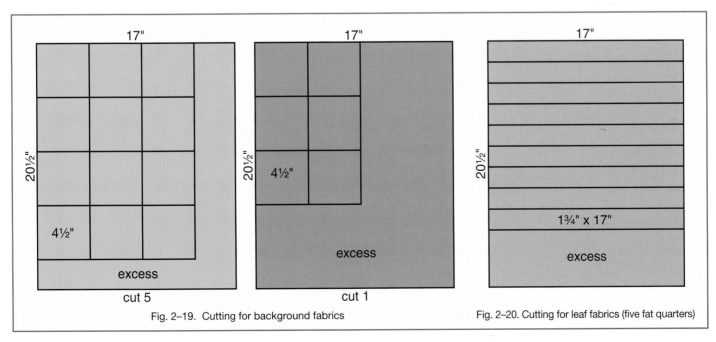

Fig. 2–19. Cutting for background fabrics

Fig. 2–20. Cutting for leaf fabrics (five fat quarters)

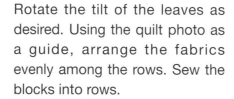

strips for a total of 22 pairs of strips.

Fig. 2–21. Sew leaf strips together in pairs.

3. Arrange three fusible web leaves on the wrong side of each set of strips, aligning the ends of each leaf with the strip seam. Fuse the web shapes to the fabric, following the manufacturer's instructions. Cut around each leaf on the traced line. You will have a total of 66 leaves.

4. Fuse one leaf diagonally to each 4½" background square, centering the leaf on the background (fig. 2–22). Use a narrow zigzag stitch and either matching or contrasting thread to appliqué each leaf in place. (For hand appliqué, trace 66 leaves, adding a turn-under allowance by eye.)

5. Arrange the blocks in six rows, each containing 11 blocks.

Rotate the tilt of the leaves as desired. Using the quilt photo as a guide, arrange the fabrics evenly among the rows. Sew the blocks into rows.

6. Measure the leaf rows and trim the three 1½" strips to match. Sew one strip between each pair of leaf rows (fig. 2–23). Press the seam allowances toward the vertical strip. Trim the two 2½" strips to match and sew them between the three sets of leaf rows. Press the seam allowances toward the vertical strips.

7. Referring to the quilt assembly diagram, measure the length of the quilt and cut two border

strips to match. Sew to the sides of the quilt. Press the seam allowances toward the border. Repeat for the top and bottom borders.

8. Mark the quilting design on the quilt top. We quilted around each leaf. In the vertical strips and the border, we used invisible thread to quilt a design resembling bamboo sticks.

9. Layer the quilt top with backing and batting. Quilt by hand or by machine. Make the binding by sewing the 2¼" fabric strips into one continuous strip. Use your favorite method to bind your quilt.

Fig. 2–22. Fuse the leaves to the background squares. Make 66.

Fig. 2–23. Quilt assembly

Bamboo Grove
Table Runner

Table runner size 14" x 53"
BAMBOO GROVE TABLE RUNNER, by Daphne Greig

This easy project is a companion piece to the BAMBOO GROVE WALL QUILT.

Cutting Instructions

■ Background blocks
From both fat quarters, cut 12 squares 4½" (fig. 2–24). You will have a total of 24 squares.

■ Leaf strips
From both fat quarters cut eight strips 1¾" x 17" (fig. 2–25). You will have a total of 16 strips.

■ Center strip
From one fat quarter cut three strips 1½" x 17".

■ Borders
Cut across the fabric to make four strips 3" x 42".

Sewing the Table Runner

1. Make a leaf template using the leaf pattern (page 32) from the BAMBOO GROVE WALL QUILT project. Use template plastic or cardboard. For machine appliqué, trace the template onto the paper

Shopping List

Amount of Fabric

2 different fat quarters for background
2 different fat quarters for leaves
1 fat quarter for center strip
½ yard for the border
1 yard of fusible web (optional)
1 yard for backing
16" x 55" piece of batting

side of fusible web 24 times, leaving about ½" between each leaf. Cut apart, leaving about ¼" around each leaf.

2. Sew two different 1¾" x 17" leaf strips together along the long edge (fig. 2–26). Press the seam allowance open. Repeat

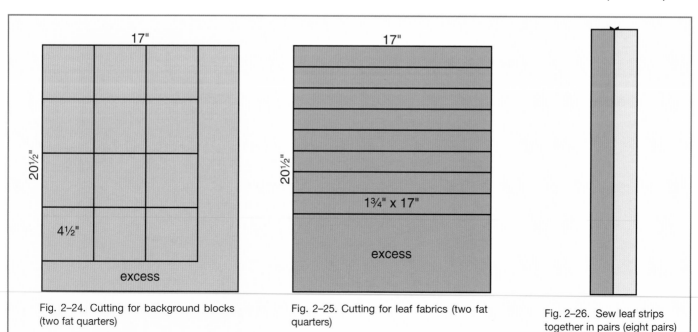

Fig. 2–24. Cutting for background blocks (two fat quarters)

17"

20½"

4½"

excess

Fig. 2–25. Cutting for leaf fabrics (two fat quarters)

17"

20½"

1¾" x 17"

excess

Fig. 2–26. Sew leaf strips together in pairs (eight pairs)

with the remaining leaf strips for a total of eight pairs of strips.

3. Arrange three fusible web leaves on the wrong side of each set of strips, aligning the ends of each leaf with the strip seam. Fuse the leaves to the fabric, following the manufacturer's instructions. Cut around each leaf on the traced line. You will have a total of 24 leaves.

4. Fuse one leaf diagonally to each 4½" background square, centering the leaf on the square (fig. 2–27).

Fig. 2–27. Block assembly (make 24)

Appliqué each leaf in place, using a narrow zigzag stitch. Use either matching or contrasting thread. (For hand appliqué, trace 24 leaves, leaving a turn-under allowance by eye. Appliqué with your favorite method.)

5. Referring to the quilt photo for color placement and leaf tilt, arrange the blocks in two rows with 12 leaves in each row. Sew the blocks in rows. Press seam allowances open.

6. Make the center strip by sewing the 1½" strips together on the short ends. Measure the leaf rows and trim the center strip to match. Sew the center strip between the two rows of leaves. Press the seam allowances toward the center strip.

7. Sew the 3" border strips together to make one continuous strip. Referring to the quilt assembly diagram (fig. 2–28, page 32), measure the long sides of the runner. From the continuous strip, cut two border strips that length. Sew these strips to the long sides of the runner. Press the seam allowances toward the border. Repeat for the short borders.

8. Cut the backing fabric into two pieces approximately 18" x 42". With a ½" seam allowance, sew the two pieces together along their short ends. Press the seam allowances to one side.

9. Layer the batting, the backing (right side up), and the table runner top (right side down). Pin around the edges and sew all around with a ¼" seam allowance, leaving a 6" opening. Trim the batting and backing even with the edges of the pieced top and clip the corners. Turn right side out, through the opening, and slipstitch the opening closed.

10. Pin-baste the layers together and quilt around the leaves and in the ditch around the border. You can also stitch ¼" from the outer edge of the table runner.

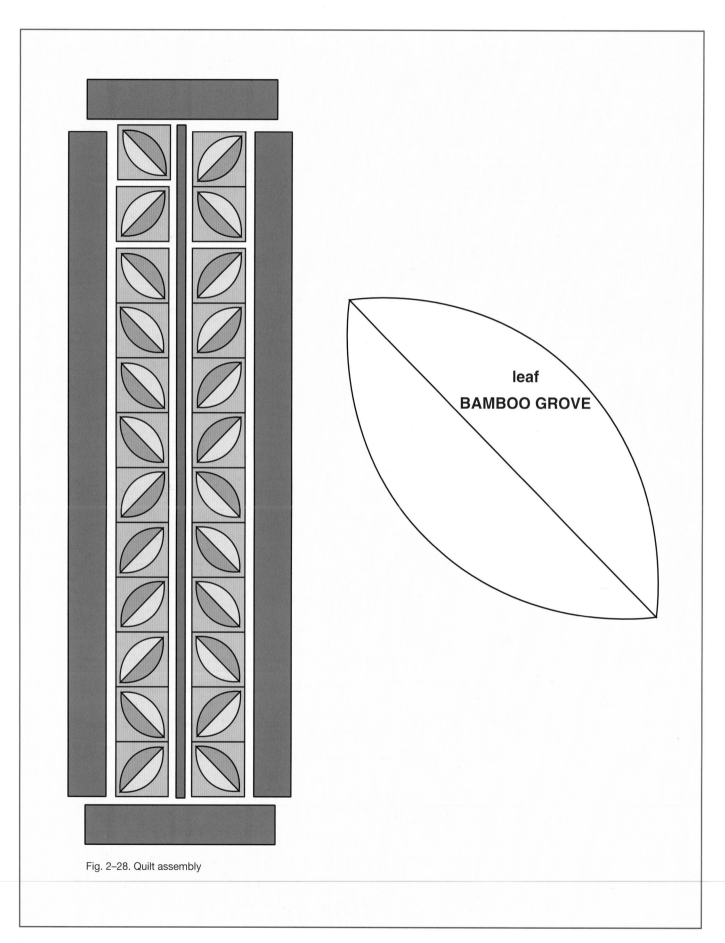

Fig. 2–28. Quilt assembly

leaf
BAMBOO GROVE

Dancing Stars

Quilt size 68" x 68"
DANCING STARS, by Susan Purney-Mark

This simple strip-pieced quilt will look lovely in many different fabric combinations. Think of using batiks or bright pastels. This is a great opportunity to use up a lot of different fat quarters; the quilt would be terrific with a scrappy look. There are two different piecing sequences to achieve the tilted star effect. Be sure to use both.

Shopping List

Amount of Fabric

17 fat quarters of assorted lights
17 fat quarters of assorted darks
4 1/4 yards for backing
72" square of batting

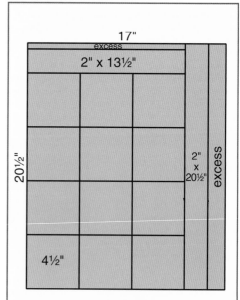

Fig. 2–29. Cutting for light background and star points (11 fat quarters)

Cutting Instructions

■ Stars and backgrounds

From each of 11 light fat quarters, cut 12 squares 4½" and two strips 2", as shown in figure 2–29. You will have a total of 132 light background squares but will use only 128 of them. The 22 light strips will be used for making star points.

In the same way, cut 11 dark fat quarters to make 132 dark background squares and 22 dark star-point strips.

From each of two light fat quarters and two dark fat quarters, cut seven strips 2" x 20½". You will have 28 more star-point strips, 14 light and 14 dark.

■ Borders

From each of two light fat quarters and two dark fat quarters, cut eight strips 2" x 20½" for borders. You will have a total of 16 light and 16 dark border strips.

■ Binding

From each of two light fat quarters and two dark fat quarters, cut 4 strips 2¼" x 20½" for binding. You will have a total of 16 binding strips.

Sewing the Quilt

1. Divide 128 light squares into two piles of 64. Sew the 64 squares in one pile to dark star-point strips, tilting each square as shown in figure 2–30.

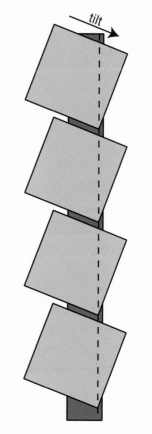

Fig. 2–30. The upper edge of each square tilts down to the right.

Star Tips

For best results, follow these important tips for sewing your star points.

■ Sew light squares on dark strips and dark squares on light strips.

■ Be sure to tilt each square in the correct direction, as shown in the figures.

■ The stitching line should not start past the halfway point on the top edge of the square and should not end past the bottom corner of the square.

■ Space the squares carefully along the strips. You should be able to fit four on the longer strips and three on the shorter strips.

2. Trim the excess fabric from the squares to match the strips (fig. 2–31). Press the seam allowances toward the strips, then trim the strips even with the squares (fig. 2–32). Cut the strips between the squares. Make 64 star-point units.

3. Using the 64 squares in the second pile, repeat step 2, but tilt the squares down to the left (fig. 2–33). Trim and press as before.

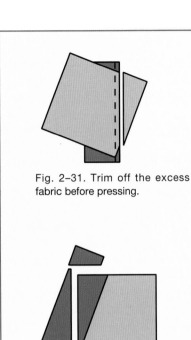

Fig. 2–31. Trim off the excess fabric before pressing.

Fig. 2–32. Trim the strips even with the squares.

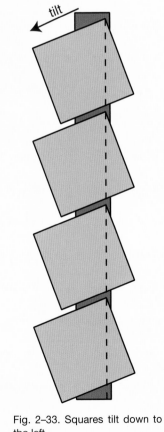

Fig. 2–33. Squares tilt down to the left.

You now have 64 units whose dark star points tilt to the left and 64 that tilt to the right (fig. 2–34).

4. Repeat steps 1–3 with the dark squares and light strips. You now have 64 units whose light star points tilt to the left and 64 pointing to the right (fig. 2–35).

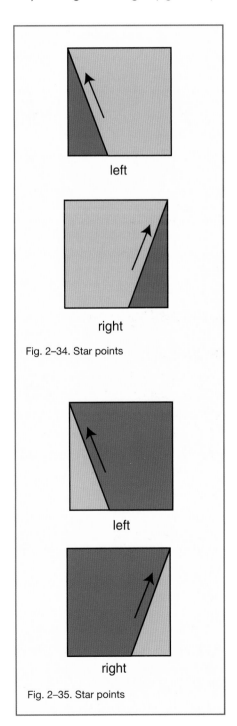

left

right

Fig. 2–34. Star points

left

right

Fig. 2–35. Star points

5. Referring to the block assembly diagram (fig. 2–36), join four star-point units of the same value together. The star blocks should measure 8½" square. You will have 16 blocks of each type, for a total of 64 blocks.

6. Arrange the blocks as shown in figure 2–37, alternating the blocks and rotating them as needed. Sew the blocks into rows and sew the rows together.

7. Alternating fabrics, join four light border strips together with 45-degree seams to make one border strip. Make a total of four light border strips. Repeat to make four dark border strips. Measure the length of the quilt top and cut two dark border strips that length. Sew the dark strips to the sides of the quilt top. Press the seam allowances toward the border strips.

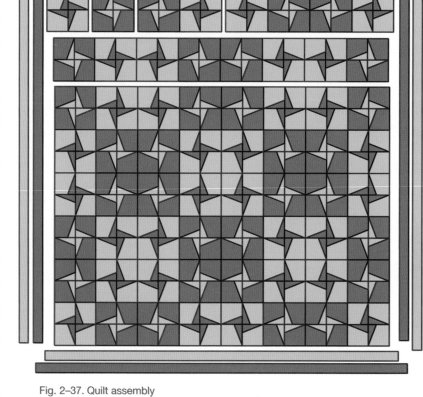

Fig. 2–37. Quilt assembly

8. Measure the width of the quilt, including the side borders, and cut two light strips that length. Sew the light strips to the top and the bottom edges of the quilt top. Press the seam allowances toward the border strips. Add the outer border in the same manner but reversing the light and dark fabric placement.

9. Mark your quilting design on the quilt top. We used an angular stippling design in between the stars and stitched in the ditch around the seams of the star points.

10. Layer the quilt with backing and batting and then quilt by hand or by machine. Make the binding with the 2¼" strips. Bind the quilt, using your favorite method. We alternated the color of the binding strips to continue the light/dark variation from the border.

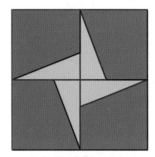
left tilt, make 16

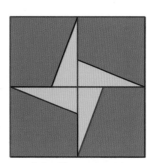
right tilt, make 16

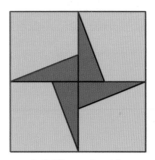
left tilt, make 16

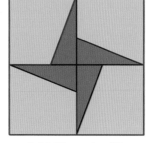
right tilt, make 16

Fig. 2–36. Star block assembly

Green Tea

Quilt size 47½" x 57"
GREEN TEA, by Daphne Greig

Showcase large-scale prints for the "Tea" blocks in this vertical row quilt. A variety of subtle background prints adds movement to the quilt. Our tea is green but you might like rose hip tea with red and pink rose prints.

Shopping List

Amount of Fabric

Light prints — 6 different fat quarters
(2 for block backgrounds, 2 for spacers
& 2 for vertical sashing)
Green prints — 4 different fat quarters for tea blocks
1 fat quarter for accent sashing
1 ³⁄₈ yards for border & binding
3 yards for backing (pieced horizontally)
52" x 61" piece of batting

Cutting Instructions

■ Light (block backgrounds)
From each of two fat quarters, cut 16 rectangles 2¾" x 4" and eight squares 3⅛" (fig. 2–38).

You will have a total of 32 rectangles and 16 squares.

■ Light (spacers)
From each of two fat quarters, cut 10 rectangles 3½" x 8½" (fig. 2–39). You will have a total of 20 rectangles.

■ Light (vertical sashing)
From one fat quarter, cut nine strips 1" x 20½". From one fat quarter, cut 15 strips 1" x 20½".

■ Green Prints (Tea blocks)
From each of four fat quarters, cut eight squares 2¾", four rectangles 4" x 8½", and four squares 3⅛" (fig. 2–40). You will have 32 squares 2 3/4", 16 rectangles, and 16 squares 3⅛".

■ Accent (sashing & inner border)
From the accent fat quarter, cut 17 strips 1" x 20½".

■ Border & binding
Cut across the fabric to make six strips 5" wide for the border and six strips 2¼" wide for the binding.

Sewing the Quilt

1. To make half-square triangle units, you will need 16 each of the

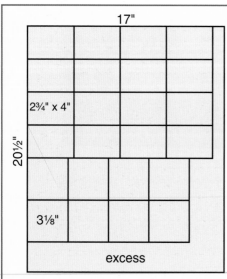

Fig. 2–38. Cutting for block backgrounds (two fat quarters)

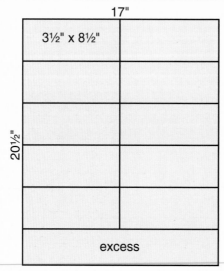

Fig. 2–39. Cutting for spacers (two fat quarters)

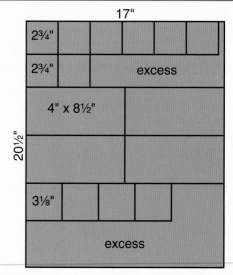

Fig. 2–40. Cutting for green prints (four fat quarters)

light print and green print 3⅛" squares. Mark a diagonal line on the wrong side of each light print square. Layer pairs of light and green print squares right sides together. Sew ¼" on each side of the line. Cut along the line and press seam allowances toward the green print. Trim units to measure 2¾" square (fig. 2–41). Make 32 units.

2. Referring to the block assembly diagram (fig. 2–42), piece 16 blocks. Use the same light and green prints throughout a single block. Each block should measure 8½" square.

3. Sew 1" x 20½" sashing strips of the same light fabric together to make one continuous strip. Repeat with the sashing strips of the other light fabric, then the accent fabric. Press all seam allowances open.

4. Referring to figure 2–43, arrange and sew four vertical rows of tea blocks and spacers. Measure the length of the rows. Cut the sashing and accent strips into eight light strips and five accent strips to match that length. Sew these strips between the rows of tea blocks and on each side.

5. Measure the width of the quilt. Cut and sew accent strips to the top and the bottom of the quilt top.

6. Sew the border strips together into one long strip with 45 degree seams. Measure the length of the quilt and cut two border strips that length. Sew to the sides of the quilt. Press the seam allowances toward the border. Repeat for the top and bottom borders.

7. Mark your quilting design on the quilt. We quilted two double rows of stitching in the spacers and quilted evenly spaced vertical and diagonal lines in the green teas.

8. Layer the quilt with backing and batting then quilt by hand or by machine. Sew the 2¼" strips together to make the binding. Use your favorite method to bind the quilt.

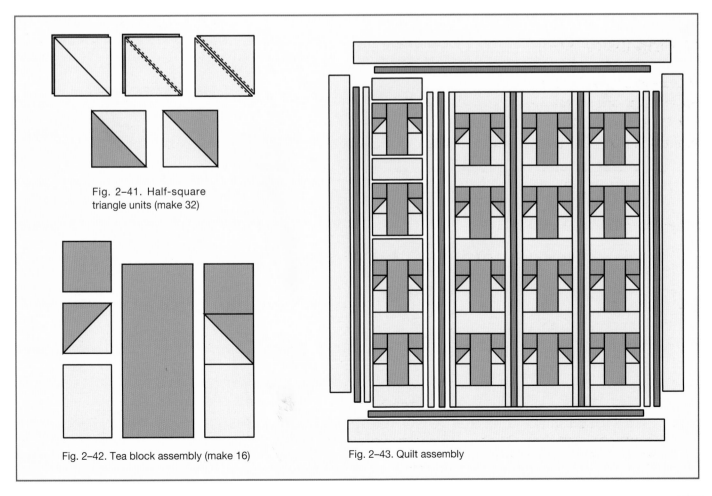

Fig. 2–41. Half-square triangle units (make 32)

Fig. 2–42. Tea block assembly (make 16)

Fig. 2–43. Quilt assembly

Woven Squares
Table Runner

Quilt size 17" x 50"
WOVEN SQUARES TABLE RUNNER, by Susan Purney-Mark

Use a coordinated pack of fat quarters from your favorite shop or a collection from your stash. You could make one table runner for each season of the year. A table runner is also a great idea for gift giving. This project includes three different blocks plus the setting triangles.

Cutting Instructions

■ Light
From one fat quarter, cut 32 squares 2½" (fig. 2–44).

■ Medium light
From one fat quarter, cut 10 squares 2½" and six squares 4½" (fig. 2–45).

Shopping List

Amount of Fabric

1 fat quarter of light fabric
1 fat quarter of medium light fabric
1 fat quarter of medium fabric
1 fat quarter of medium dark fabric
1 fat quarter of dark fabric
1 fat quarter for binding
1 yard for backing
21" x 54" piece of batting

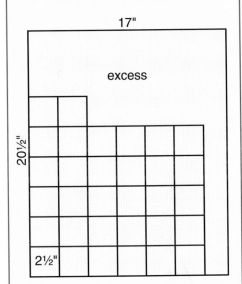

Fig. 2–44. Cutting for light fabric (one fat quarter)

■ Medium
From one fat quarter, you'll make three cuts. For the first one, cut three strips 5" (fig. 2–46).

For the second cut, refer to figure 2–47. Cut the strips into triangles as shown, by using the 45-degree line on a rotary-cutting

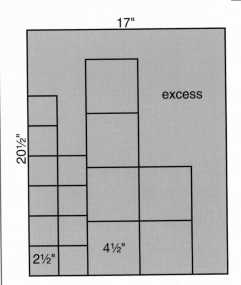

Fig. 2–45. Cutting for medium light fabric (one fat quarter)

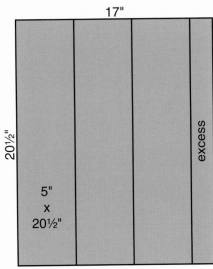

Fig. 2–46. First cut for medium fabric (one fat quarter)

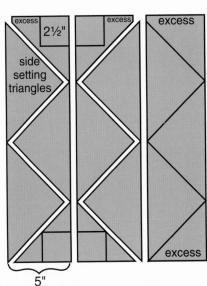

Fig. 2–47. Second and third cuts for the medium fat quarter

ruler. You will have nine triangles but will use only eight. These are the setting triangles for the sides of the table runner.

For the third cut, cut four squares 2½" from the remaining small triangles. There will be two small triangles left over.

■ Medium dark
From one fat quarter, cut six squares 2½" and 14 rectangles 2½" x 4½" (fig. 2–48).

■ Dark
From one fat quarter, cut 16 squares 2½" and 12 rectangles 2½" x 4½" (fig. 2–49).

■ Binding
Cut eight strips 1½" x 20½".

Sewing the Table Runner

1. Referring to the block assembly diagram (fig. 2–50), make six of blocks 1 and 2 and four of block 3.

Press seam allowances open. Block should measure 6½" x 6½".

2. Arrange the blocks and setting triangles, referring to the quilt assembly diagram (fig. 2–51). Sew together rows of blocks and triangles, and then join the rows to complete the runner.

3. Mark your quilting design on the runner. We quilted around each block then used an interlocking circle design on top of each block. The setting triangles can be quilted in diagonal lines.

4. Cut the backing into two pieces approximately 20" x 28". With a ½" seam allowance, sew the two pieces together along their short ends. Press the seam allowances to one side.

5. Layer the runner with backing and batting and quilt by hand or by machine. Use your favorite method to bind the table runner.

Fig. 2–51. Quilt assembly

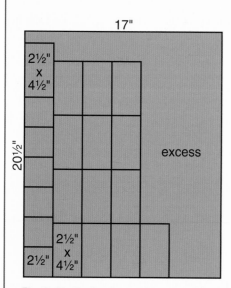

Fig. 2–48. Cutting for medium dark fabric (one fat quarter)

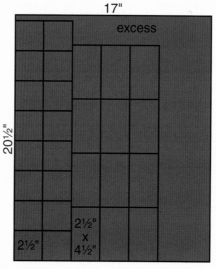

Fig. 2–49. Cutting for dark fabric (one fat quarter)

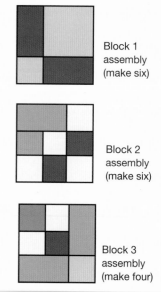

Block 1 assembly (make six)

Block 2 assembly (make six)

Block 3 assembly (make four)

Fig. 2–50.

Another Colorway
Woven Squares Table Runner

Quilt size 17" x 50"
WOVEN SQUARES TABLE RUNNER
by Susan Purney-Mark

Empress Tiles

Quilt size 72" x 96"
EMPRESS TILES, by Susan Purney-Mark

A carpet in a hotel near where we live inspired this quilt. It's an easy technique in which every block is slightly different. You can make the quilt as large as you like by adding or subtracting blocks. Have fun with color selection and consider subtle value changes when selecting your fabric. Think of using all batiks, floral prints, or Christmas fabrics.

Cutting Instructions

■ **Triangles**
Layer four to six fat quarters together at a time for ease of cutting, and cut four strips 4½" x 17" (fig. 2–52). Repeat to make 144 strips.

■ **Binding**
Cut leftovers from fat quarters to make strips 2¼".

Note: When you cut the strips into triangles, vary the angles by 10 to 45 degrees (estimated by eye) to make the design more interesting. Cut at least six but no more than eight triangles across each stack. The triangles need not be identical. Cut, sew, and press one entire group of strips before proceeding to the next group.

Organizing, Layering and Cutting

Shopping List

Amount of Fabric

36 fat quarters* (half light, half dark) for triangles
5⅞ yards for backing
Leftover strips from fat quarters for binding
76" x 100" piece of batting

*You could also use scraps that measure 4½" x 17" (minimum).

1. Select four light and four dark strips. Layer them, alternating light and dark (fig. 2–53). Repeat until all strips are placed into groups.

2. Starting near the left edge of the group, make a diagonal cut through all the layers (fig. 2–54, page 46).

3. Place the rotary-cutting ruler ¼" away from the end of the diagonal cut and make another

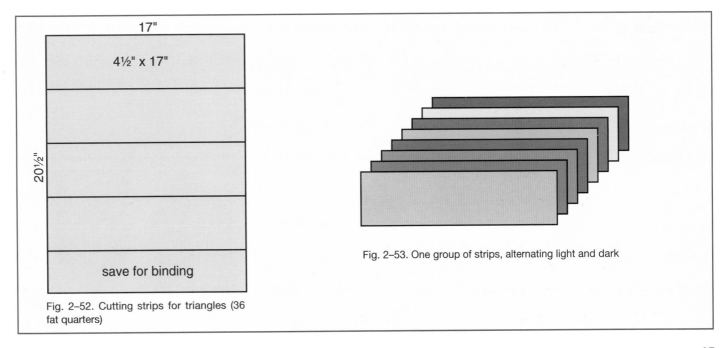

Fig. 2–52. Cutting strips for triangles (36 fat quarters)

```
              17"
   ┌─────────────────────┐
   │    4½" x 17"         │
   ├─────────────────────┤
   │                     │
   ├─────────────────────┤
20½"│                     │
   ├─────────────────────┤
   │                     │
   ├─────────────────────┤
   │   save for binding  │
   └─────────────────────┘
```

Fig. 2–53. One group of strips, alternating light and dark

Making a Practice Block with Three Fabrics

Making a practice block before you cut your quilt fabrics will let you test the angle of your cuts and your triangle piecing. Follow the pattern instructions to cut and sew your test block.

From each of three contrasting scrap fabrics, cut a strip 4½" x 17". Layer the strips and cut the triangles. You can vary the angle of the cuts by eye, but be precise when you place your ¼" imaginary line. It will help you piece the triangles accurately. Keeping the cut triangles in order from left to right, arrange them in three rows, mixing the colors at random. Sew, measure, and trim each triangle row to 4½" x 12½".

If your rows are short in either direction, check the size of your seam allowances and the angle of your triangles. You may find it helpful to make the first cut, on the left, at a fairly narrow angle.

Sew the three rows into a block. It should measure 12½" x 12½".

diagonal cut through all the layers. Picturing an imaginary line, as shown in figure 2-55, can help you place the ruler. You may want to pencil in a dot on the ¼" line to help you align the ruler. Again, the angle of the cut should be between 10 and 45 degrees. Continue cutting across the group of strips, alternating the direction of each cut (fig. 2–56).

Fig. 2–54. First cut. Cut through all layers.

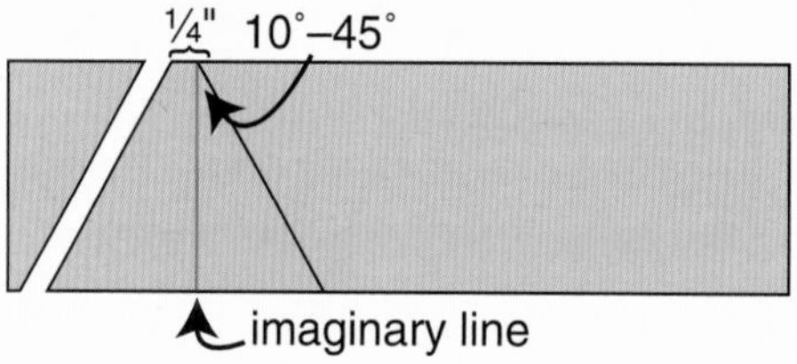

Fig. 2–55. Second cut

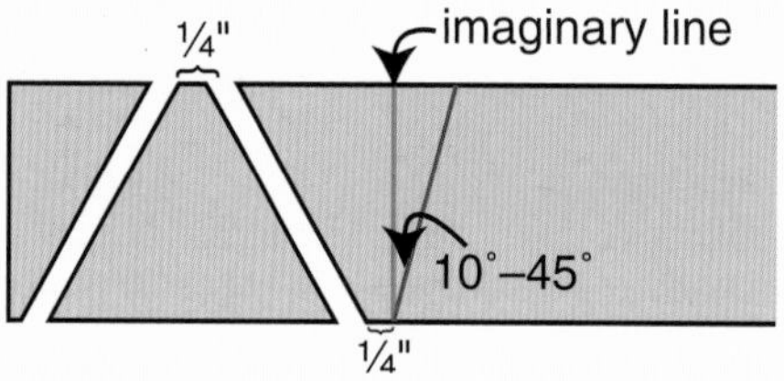

Fig. 2–56. Third cut

Re-arranging Triangles

4. Keeping the triangles stacked in their cut layers, carefully re-arrange the triangles for sewing, as follows:

Working from the left, leave the first stack of triangles alone.
a. From the second stack, move the first triangle to the bottom of the pile.
b. From the third stack, move the top two triangles to the bottom of the pile.
c. From the fourth stack, move the top three triangles to the bottom of the pile (fig. 2–57).

5. Continue this sequence, moving one additional triangle for each subsequent stack, until you reach the end of the row of triangles. It is important not to disturb the sequence of triangles across the row or the sequence of triangles in each stack.

We recommend that you work with one group of strips at a time and keep the stacked triangles on a flat tray or small mat to move them from the cutting area to the sewing area.

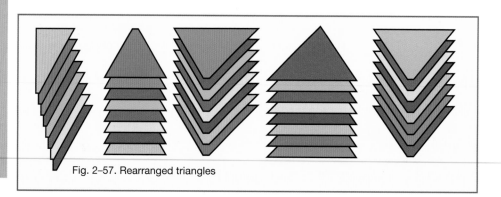

Fig. 2–57. Rearranged triangles

Sewing the Triangles

6. Sew the triangles from the top of each stack together. The flat tip at the top of each triangle and the overlap at the bottom will help with alignment for sewing. Sew with a ¼" seam allowance (fig. 2–58). Finger-press each seam allowance toward the triangle you have just added. Continue adding triangles in this manner until you have reached the end of the row. Press the entire row.

7. In the same manner, sew the triangles together for each row. The triangles will alternate light and dark along the row. You will have eight rows, and each row will be unique. Repeat the steps to sew the remaining groups of strips.

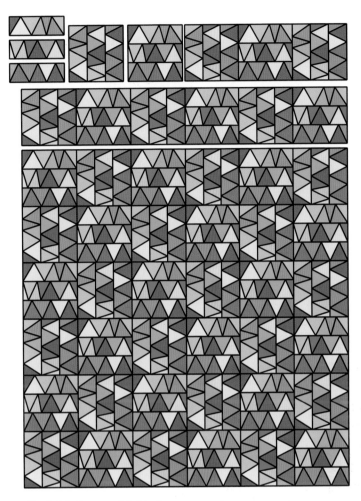

Fig. 2–60. One possible block arrangement

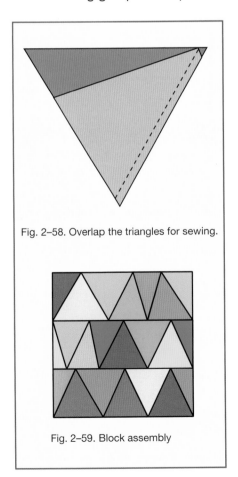

Fig. 2–58. Overlap the triangles for sewing.

Fig. 2–59. Block assembly

Sewing the Quilt

8. Make sure all rows are well pressed. Trim each row to 12½" long. Trim some rows at the beginning and some rows at the end to create more variety. Join three rows to form a 12½" block with the tops of the dark triangles all pointing in one direction (fig. 2–59). Make all strips into blocks.

Note: The points of the triangles do not match with those in the previous row. Some of the triangle points may be cut off, and the overall effect will be relaxed.

9. Arrange the blocks as desired to make the quilt top. There are many possible layout combinations. One option is shown in figure 2–60.

10. Mark your quilting design on the quilt. We quilted a straight grid design with random diagonal lines on our quilt. Other possibilities include leaf patterns, florals, or cable designs.

11. Layer the quilt with backing and batting and then quilt by hand or by machine. Use your favorite method to bind the quilt with the 2¼" strips.

Layered Pinwheels

Quilt size 58" x 78"

LAYERED PINWHEELS, by Daphne Greig

Rows of spinning pinwheels march across this quilt. Choose light fabrics for the background, medium and dark colors for the pinwheels, and a color that contrasts with both the background and the pinwheels for the lattice (gold).

Cutting Instructions

■ **Templates**

Use template plastic or light-weight cardboard to make A and B templates from the patterns on page 51.

■ **Light (block backgrounds)**

From each of five fat quarters, cut 28 squares 3⅜" (fig. 2–61). You will need 140 squares. Cut each square in half diagonally for a total of 280 triangles.

■ **Gold lattice**

From each of nine fat quarters, cut three strips 3" x 20½" and two strips 3⅜" x 20½". From each 3" strip, cut five A patches. From one 3⅜" strip of each color, cut one A patch (144 A total). From the 3⅜" strips, cut 72 squares 3⅜". Cut each square in half diagonally (fig. 2–62).

■ **Pinwheels**

From each of the eight fat quarters, cut five strips 3" x 20½".

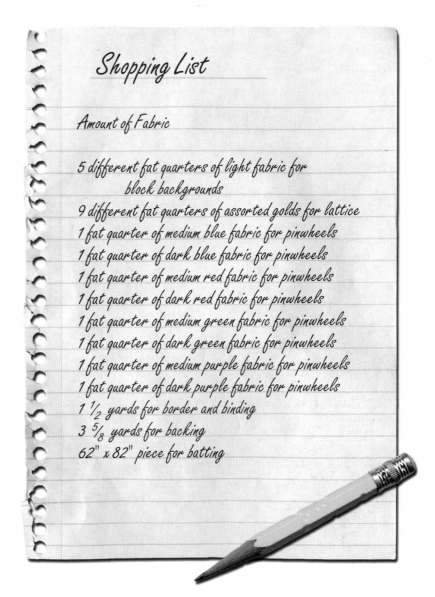

Shopping List

Amount of Fabric

5 different fat quarters of light fabric for block backgrounds
9 different fat quarters of assorted golds for lattice
1 fat quarter of medium blue fabric for pinwheels
1 fat quarter of dark blue fabric for pinwheels
1 fat quarter of medium red fabric for pinwheels
1 fat quarter of dark red fabric for pinwheels
1 fat quarter of medium green fabric for pinwheels
1 fat quarter of dark green fabric for pinwheels
1 fat quarter of medium purple fabric for pinwheels
1 fat quarter of dark purple fabric for pinwheels
1 ½ yards for border and binding
3 ⅝ yards for backing
62" x 82" piece for batting

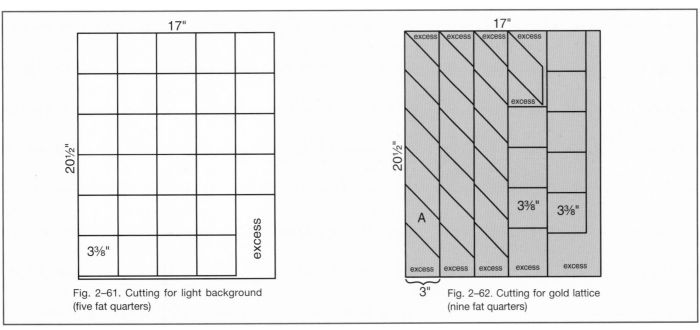

Fig. 2–61. Cutting for light background (five fat quarters)

Fig. 2–62. Cutting for gold lattice (nine fat quarters)

Use template B to cut 18 patches from the strips, for a total of 144 B (fig. 2–63).

■ **Border & binding**
Cutting across the fabric width, cut seven 4½" strips for the border and eight 2¼" strips for the binding.

Sewing the Quilt

1. Referring to the piecing diagram in figure 2–64, make 35 blocks, as follows: Use the same fabric for the A patches in each block and arrange the light and dark colors as shown. Press open the seam allowances that join the four star-point units. Each block will measure 10½" square.

2. Arrange the blocks in rows, placing the colors as shown in the quilt photo. Sew the blocks together in rows then sew the rows together. Press all these seam allowances open for a flatter quilt top.

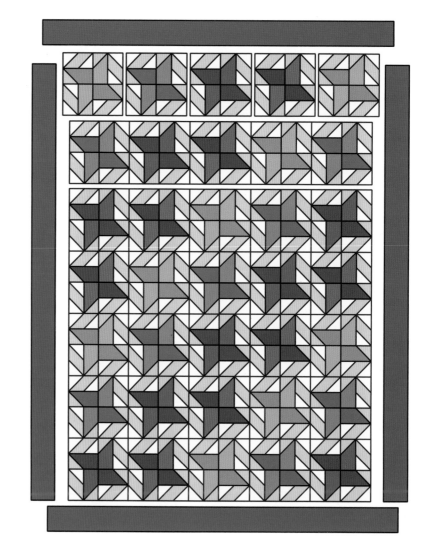

Fig. 2–65. Quilt assembly

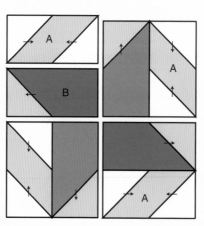

Fig. 2–63. Cutting for pinwheels (eight fat quarters)

Fig. 2–64. Block assembly (make 35). Press seam allowances as shown by the arrows.

3. Join the 4½" border strips to make one long strip. Measure the length of the quilt and cut two pieces that length from the strip. Sew them to the sides of the quilt. Measure the width of the quilt and cut two pieces that length. Sew these to the top and bottom (fig. 2–65). Press the seam allowances toward the border.

4. Layer the quilt top with the backing and the batting. Quilt ½" inside each pinwheel and in the ditch around the A patches in each block. Make the binding with the 2¼" strips. Bind the quilt, using your favorite method.

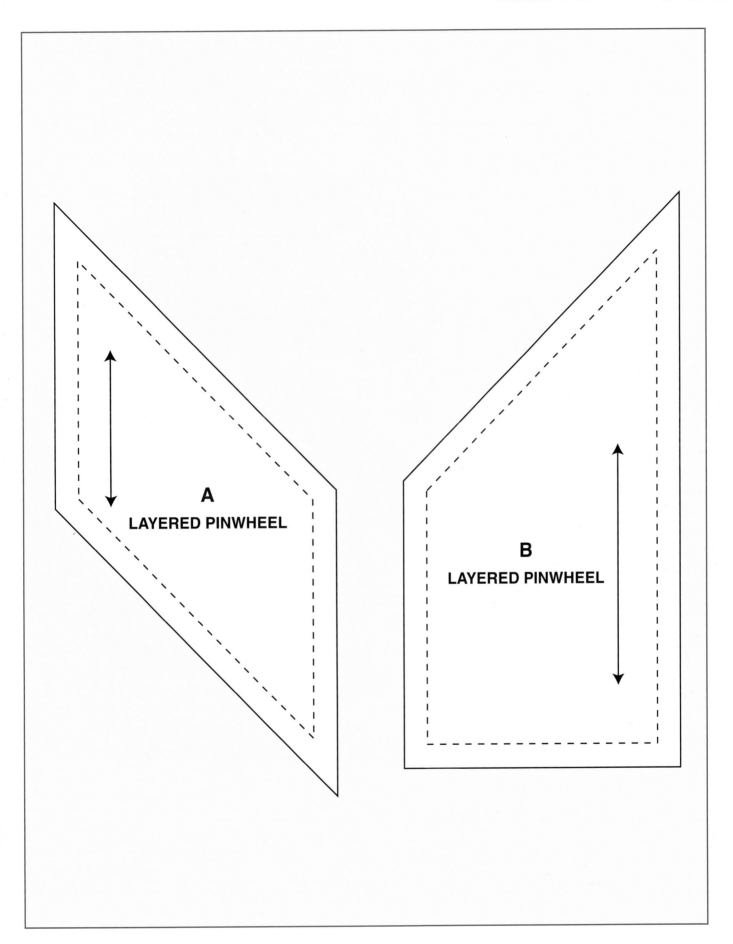

A
LAYERED PINWHEEL

B
LAYERED PINWHEEL

Many Rising Stars

Quilt size 60" x 60"

MANY RISING STARS, by Daphne Greig

These large blocks are quick to sew. Before you know it, you'll have the whole quilt top finished. This project includes some speedy techniques for sewing the star points. Try bright and dramatic colors. The quilt works equally well with soft color changes.

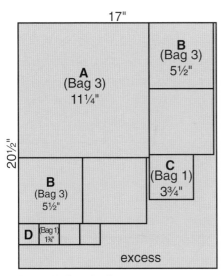

Fig. 2–66. Cut nine fat quarters.

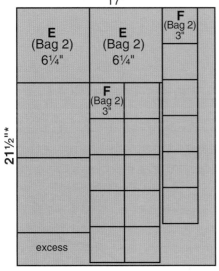

Fig. 2–67. These two fat quarters must be 21½", or you will need a second fat quarter of each fabric.

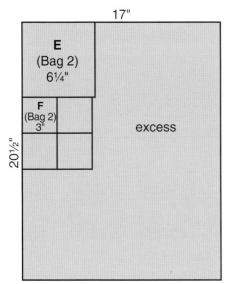

Fig. 2–68. Cut one fat quarter.

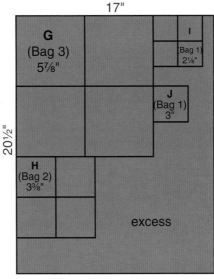

Fig. 2–69. Cut nine fat quarters.

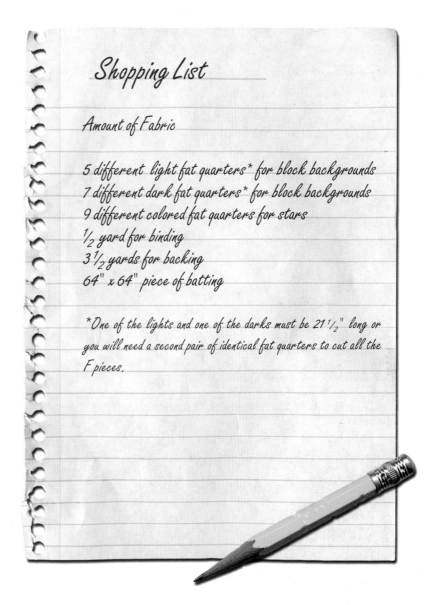

Shopping List

Amount of Fabric

5 different light fat quarters* for block backgrounds
7 different dark fat quarters* for block backgrounds
9 different colored fat quarters for stars
½ yard for binding
3½ yards for backing
64" x 64" piece of batting

*One of the lights and one of the darks must be 21½" long or you will need a second pair of identical fat quarters to cut all the F pieces.

Cutting Instructions

Cut squares from the fat quarters, as shown in the cutting diagrams. Pin same-sized squares together and label them with their corresponding letters. Arrange the squares into three separate groups. Place each group into a large zipper-topped bag. Label the bags 1 (inner star), 2 (middle star points), and 3 (outer star points). The cutting chart on page 54 and accompanying cutting diagrams will tell you which pieces go in each bag.

Cutting

Fabric	Squares	Size	Bag
5 dark and 4 light fat quarters *(fig. 2–66)*	1 A	11¼"	3
	4 B	5½"	3
	1 C	3¾"	1
	4 D	1¾"	1
1 dark and 1 light fat quarter* *(fig. 2–67)*	4 E	6¼"	2
	16 F	3"	2
1 dark fat quarter *(fig. 2–68)*	1 E	6¼"	2
	4 F	3"	2
9 fat quarters for stars *(fig. 2–69)*	4 G	5⅞"	3
	4 H	3⅜"	2
	4 I	2⅛"	1
	1 J	3"	1
Binding	7 strips 2¼" x 42"		

*These fat quarters for E and F need to be 21½" long. Otherwise, you will need another pair of fat quarters of the same fabrics to finish cutting the F pieces.

Sewing Inner Stars

1. Working with bag 1, arrange nine sets of squares, each containing one J, four I the same color as the J, one light or dark C, and four D the same color as C.

2. Select one set of squares and mark a diagonal line from corner to corner on the wrong side of the four I squares. Place two I squares on the C square, right sides together. Sew ¼" from each side of the line. Cut along the line and finger press the small triangles away from the large triangle (fig. 2–70).

3. Place one marked I square on one of the units from the previous step, right sides together, and sew ¼" from each side of the marked line. Cut along the line and finger press the small triangles. Repeat for the other unit. You now have four flying geese units (3" x 1¾") to use for the star points (fig. 2–71).

4. Arrange and sew one sawtooth star with the four flying geese units and one J and four D squares from the same set (fig. 2–72). The star should measure 5½" square. Repeat with the other eight sets of squares to make nine sawtooth (inner) stars.

Adding Middle Star Points

5. Working with the squares in bag 2, arrange nine sets of squares. Each set should contain four H all the same color, one background E, and four F the same color as E. Keep the background the same for each block, either all light or all dark.

6. As before, for each block, make four flying geese units with the H and E squares. The units should measure 3" x 5½".

7. Sew the flying geese units and the F squares to the inner stars

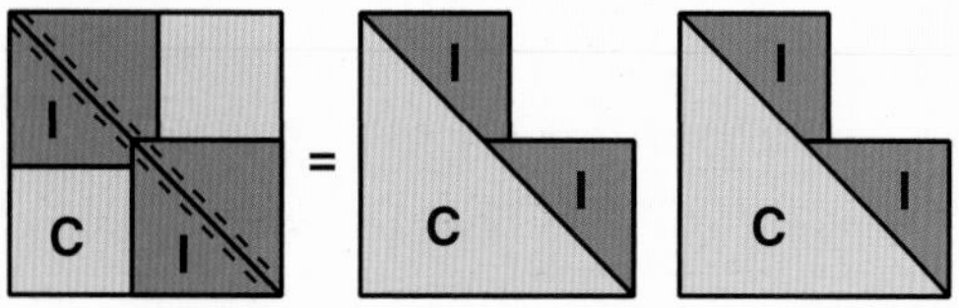

Fig. 2–70. Sew and cut the I squares and C squares.

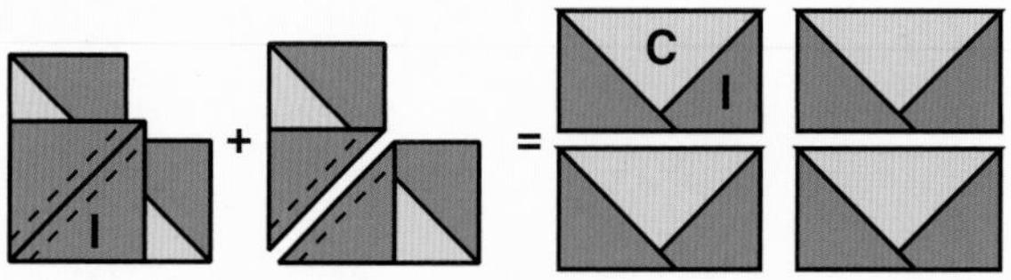

Fig. 2–71. Make four flying geese units for the star points.

(fig. 2–73). Make nine blocks measuring 10½" square.

Adding Outer Star Points

8. Working with the squares in bag 3, arrange nine sets of squares. The outer flying geese star points and the inner star should be the same color. Each set should contain four G all the same color, one A, and four B the same color as A.

9. Make flying geese units with the G and A squares. The units should measure 5½" x 10½".

10. Sew the flying geese units and the B squares to the middle stars (fig. 2–74). Make nine blocks measuring 20½" square.

Assemble the quilt

11. Arrange the blocks in rows, alternating blocks with dark and light backgrounds. Sew the blocks together in rows then sew the rows together (fig. 2–75, page 56). Press all the seam allowances open for a flatter quilt top.

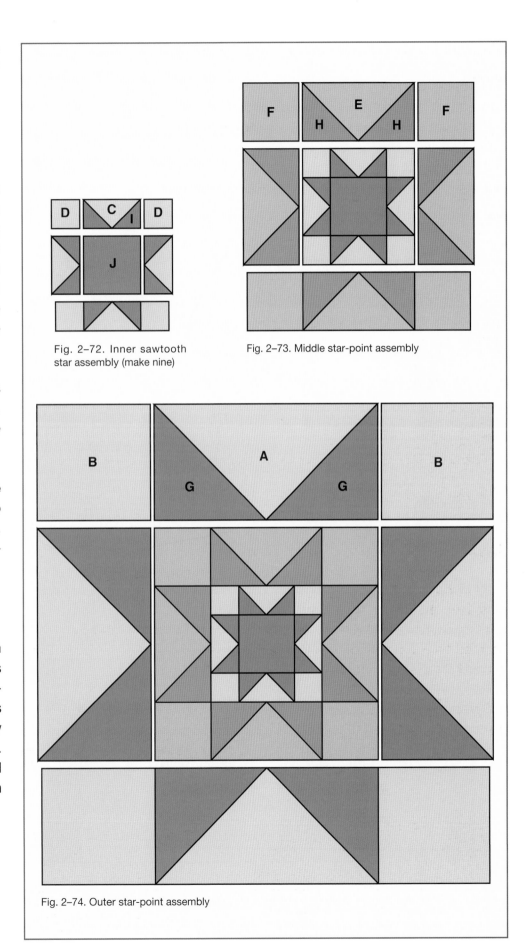

Fig. 2–72. Inner sawtooth star assembly (make nine)

Fig. 2–73. Middle star-point assembly

Fig. 2–74. Outer star-point assembly

12. Mark your quilting design on the quilt. We machine quilted the block backgrounds in a series of concentric squares to fill the spaces. The star points were not quilted so they would stand up from the background.

13. Layer the quilt with backing and batting and quilt by hand or by machine. Use the binding strips and your favorite method to bind the raw edges of the quilt.

Fig. 2–75. Quilt assembly

Snails in My Garden

Quilt size 34" x 34"

SNAILS IN MY GARDEN, by Daphne Greig

On the West Coast, we often have a battle with slugs and snails nibbling on our gardens. So we created this wall quilt in which the snails stay in their place and the flowers bloom happily beside them. Three-dimensional petals give our flowers a playful look.

Shopping List

Amount of Fabric

4 different fat quarters for Snail's Trail blocks
   & Flower block triangles
2 fat quarters for Flower block background
   & Flower centers (light)
1 fat quarter for leaves
2 fat quarters for flower petals
⅝ yard for border & binding
1 yard for backing
21" square of very thin batting for flower petals & centers
36" square of batting

Cutting Instructions

■ Snail's Trail blocks &
  Flower block triangles
Referring to figure 2–76 and the chart, cut four fat quarters.

■ Templates
Use template plastic or lightweight cardboard to make templates from the patterns on page 61. Do not add turn-under allowances to the templates.

■ Flower block backgrounds
  & flower centers
From one fat quarter, cut four squares 7⅝". From another fat quarter, cut one square 7⅝". Trace the flower center template five times and cut the circles, adding a ³⁄₁₆" turn-under allowance when you cut the fabric circles.

■ Leaves
On one fat quarter, trace the leaf template 20 times and cut the leaves, adding a ³⁄₁₆" turn-under allowance.

■ Flower petals
From each of two fat quarters, cut 20 flower petals for the flower front and lining with the petal template. Add a ¼" seam allowance when you cut the petals.

■ Thin batting
Cut five flower center circles. Do not add turn-under allowances. Use the petal template to cut 20 petal shapes. Add a ¼" seam allowance when you cut these pieces.

Cutting

Squares	Size	Second Cut
4 A	1¾"	—
1 B	3¾"	quarter diagonally
2 C	3⅜"	halve diagonally
1 D	6¼"	quarter diagonally
5 E	5⅞"	halve diagonally

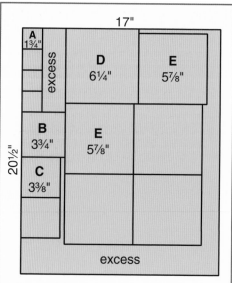

Fig. 2–76. Cutting for Snail's Trail blocks and Flower block triangles (four fat quarters)

■ Border & binding

Cut across the fabric to make four strips 2½" for the border and four strips 2¼" for the binding.

Sewing the Quilt

1. Referring to figure 2–77 and to the quilt photo, sew one A square of each color and one B, C, D, and E triangle of each color to make a block. Make four Snail's Trails blocks. They will measure 10½" square.

2. Sew one E triangle of each color to the sides of each light 7⅝" Flower block background square to make Flower blocks (fig. 2–78). Make five Flower blocks. They will measure 10½" square.

3. Use your favorite method to appliqué four leaves to each Flower block, centering the leaves on the block. Refer to the quilt picture as a guide.

4. Make the flower petals by layering one flower petal cut from batting, one flower petal for the front, right side up, and one flower petal for the lining, right side down (fig. 2–79). Sew around the layers with a ¼" seam allowance, leaving the bottom open. Trim the seam allowance to ⅛" and turn right side out. Gently press each flower petal. Make 20 petals.

5. Fold each petal along the fold line to make a narrower petal. Arrange four petals on each

Fig. 2–77. Snail's Trail block assembly (make four)

flower block, centering one petal between each pair of leaves. The petals will overlap slightly in the middle of the block. Baste the bottom raw edges to the block.

6. Make the flower centers by placing one batting circle on the wrong side of one flower center. Sew a running stitch by hand around the outside of the fabric circle and draw up the gathers, turning the seam allowance to the wrong side to cover the edge of the batting. Distribute the gathers evenly and anchor the end of the thread by sewing sev-

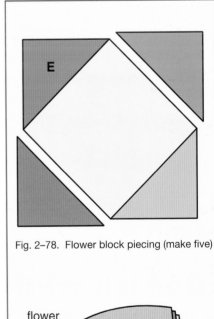

Fig. 2–78. Flower block piecing (make five)

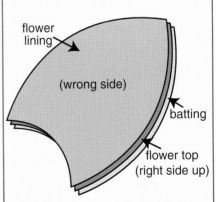

Fig. 2–79. Flower petal assembly

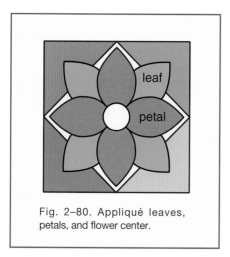

Fig. 2–80. Appliqué leaves, petals, and flower center.

inside the patches of the Snail's Trail blocks, following each color. We also quilted inside the triangle patches and leaves of the Flower blocks.

11. Layer the quilt with backing and batting then quilt by hand or by machine. You may want to tack the flower petals to the surface of the quilt. Use the 2¼" strips to bind your quilt.

eral small stitches on top of each other. Gently press the flower center. Make five (fig. 2–80).

7. Position the prepared flower center in the center of the block and machine stitch around it with invisible thread and a narrow zigzag or blind hem stitch. (The needle should take a very small bite into the flower center fabric.)

8. Arrange and sew the Snail's Trail blocks and the Flower blocks as shown in figure 2–81.

9. Measure the length of the quilt and cut two border strips to that length. Sew the borders to the sides of the quilt. Press the seam allowances toward the border strips. Repeat for the top and bottom borders.

10. Mark your quilting design on the quilt. We quilted ⅜"

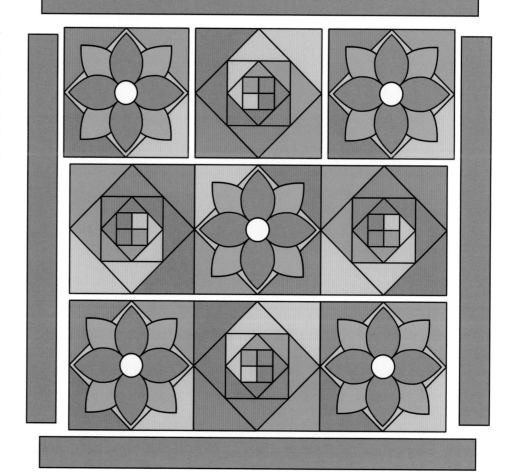

Fig. 2–81. Quilt assembly

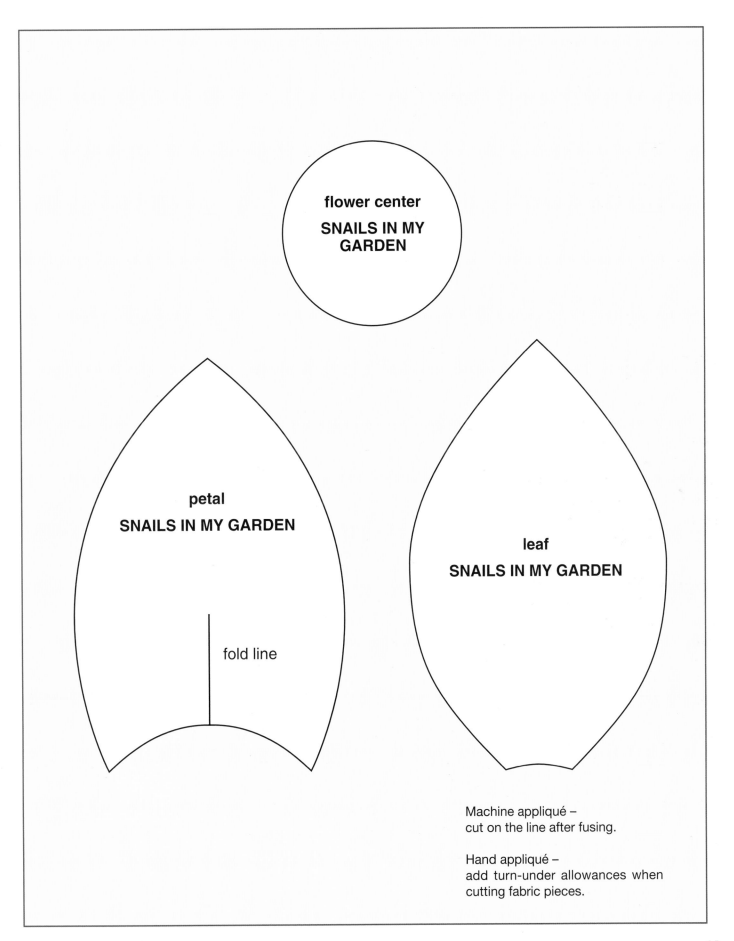

flower center
SNAILS IN MY GARDEN

petal
SNAILS IN MY GARDEN

fold line

leaf
SNAILS IN MY GARDEN

Machine appliqué –
cut on the line after fusing.

Hand appliqué –
add turn-under allowances when
cutting fabric pieces.

Cottage Country

Quilt size 29½" x 42"
COTTAGE COUNTRY, by Daphne Greig

Put on your architect's hat and build this fun row quilt. Your houses can be realistic or whimsical.

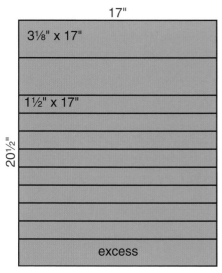

Fig. 2–82. Cutting for houses and inner and outer borders (three fat quarters)

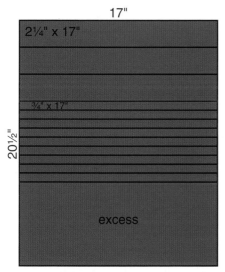

Fig. 2–83. Cutting for doors and middle border (one fat quarter)

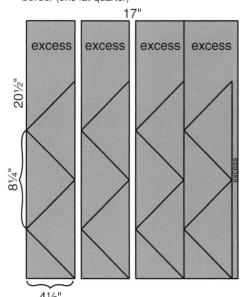

Fig. 2–84. Cutting for roofs (one fat quarter)

Shopping List

Amount of Fabric

⅝ yard of fabric for sky
1 fat quarter for chimneys
3 different fat quarters for houses & borders
1 fat quarter for doors & borders
1 fat quarter for roofs
1 fat quarter for grass
⅜ yard for binding
1⅜ yards for backing
34" x 46" piece of batting

Cutting

Strips	Size
Sky	
one strip	2" x 42" (sky strip)
two strips	1¾" x 42" (sky for chimney unit)
one strip	4⅜" x 42" (triangles)
second cut	6 squares 4⅜", cut in half diagonally
four strips	1½" x 42" (block sashing)
second cut	16 strips 1½" x 7½"
Chimneys	
two strips	1⅞" x 17"

Houses, Inner & Outer Borders *(fig. 2–82)*
Each fat quarter:

two strips	3⅛" x 17" (houses)
eight strips	1½" x 17" (borders)
second cut	4 segments 1½" x 3½", from each strip

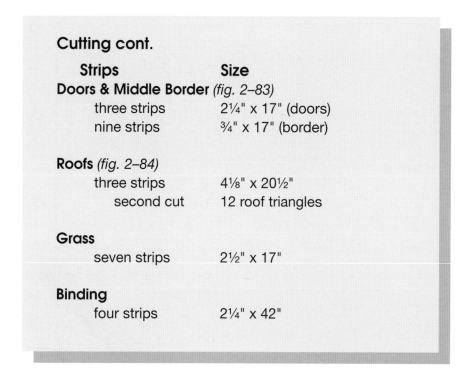

Cutting cont.

Strips	Size
Doors & Middle Border *(fig. 2–83)*	
three strips	2¼" x 17" (doors)
nine strips	¾" x 17" (border)
Roofs *(fig. 2–84)*	
three strips	4⅛" x 20½"
second cut	12 roof triangles
Grass	
seven strips	2½" x 17"
Binding	
four strips	2¼" x 42"

Sewing the Units

1. Make chimney units: Join the two chimney strips to make one long strip. Sew that strip between two 1¾" sky strips (fig. 2–85). There will be excess sky strip fabric at one end. Press the seam allowances toward the chimney strip. The pieced strip should measure 4⅜" wide. Cut six 4⅜" squares from the strip, placing the cuts to avoid the chimney seam. Cut each square in half diagonally, slanting the cuts as shown in figure 2–86.

2. Make roof units: Sew together the sky triangles, the chimney/sky units, and the roof triangles to make the roof units (fig. 2–87). Make 12, six with the chimney on the left and six with the chimney on the right. The units should measure 4" x 7½".

3. Make house units: Sew one door strip between each pair of matching house strips. Make three of these. The sewn strips should measure 7½" wide. Cut four 4" x 7½" units from each pieced strip, for a total of 12 (fig. 2–88).

4. Join the roof and house units to complete each house (fig. 2–89). Each block should measure 7½" x 7½".

Sewing the Quilt

5. Arrange the houses and the block sashing strips into four rows, each with three houses and four sashing strips (fig. 2–90). Sew the houses and strips together in each row. Press the seam allowances toward the sashing.

6. Sew the seven grass strips together end to end. Measure the house rows and cut the sky strip and four grass strips to match. Sew the house rows together with the sky strip at the top of the quilt and a grass strip below each house row. Press the seam allowances toward the strips.

7. For the inner border, join all 1½" x 3½" house fabric segments together end to end. Press the seam allowances open. Referring again to figure 2–90, measure, cut, and sew the pieced borders to the quilt top. Repeat for the middle border, using the ¾" x 17" door fabric strips. Repeat for the outer border, using the house fabric strip.

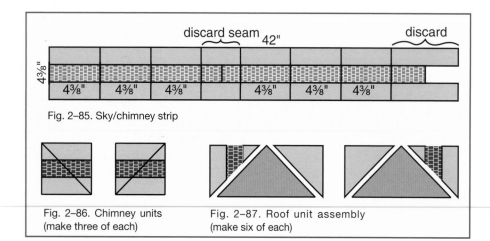

Fig. 2–85. Sky/chimney strip

Fig. 2–86. Chimney units (make three of each)

Fig. 2–87. Roof unit assembly (make six of each)

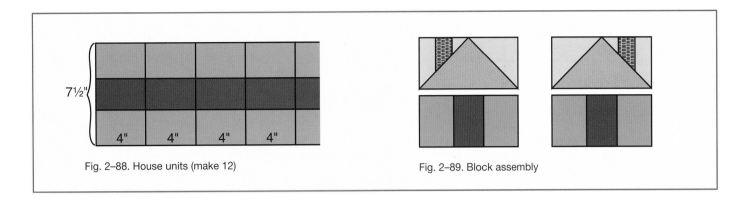

Fig. 2–88. House units (make 12)

Fig. 2–89. Block assembly

8. Mark your quilting design on the quilt. We quilted around each house and around the doors and the chimneys. We quilted a grass design in the grass strip and some clouds in the sky.

9. Layer the quilt with backing and batting and then quilt by hand or by machine. Sew the 2¼" strips together to make the binding. Bind the quilt, using your favorite method.

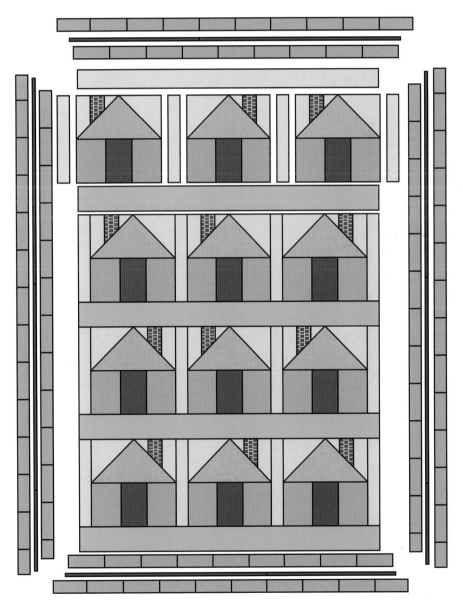

Fig. 2–90. Quilt assembly

Zigzag Stars

Quilt size 57½" x 73½"
ZIGZAG STARS, by Daphne Greig

Piece some simple stars and setting units. Select your two favorite color families to make a dramatic quilt.

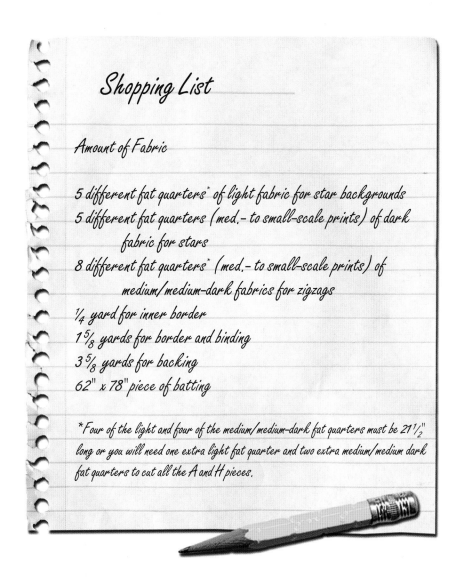

Shopping List

Amount of Fabric

5 different fat quarters* of light fabric for star backgrounds

5 different fat quarters (med.- to small-scale prints) of dark
     fabric for stars

8 different fat quarters* (med.- to small-scale prints) of
     medium/medium-dark fabrics for zigzags

¼ yard for inner border

1⅝ yards for border and binding

3⅝ yards for backing

62" x 78" piece of batting

*Four of the light and four of the medium/medium-dark fat quarters must be 21½"
long or you will need one extra light fat quarter and two extra medium/medium dark
fat quarters to cut all the A and H pieces.

Cutting Instructions

Before cutting the zigzag fat quarters, separate them into two stacks of four, dividing the medium and medium-dark fabrics evenly between the two stacks. Then cut all the patches from the yardage or fat quarters as shown in the table on page 68.

Sewing the Quilt

1. To make the flying-geese star points, mark a diagonal line, corner to corner, on the wrong side of four matching E squares. Layer two E squares right sides together with one A square (fig. 2–97, page 69). Sew ¼" on each side of the line. Cut along the line and press the small triangles away from the large triangle.

2. Layer one E square right sides together with each A/E unit. Sew ¼" on each side of the marked line. Cut along the line and press the small triangles as

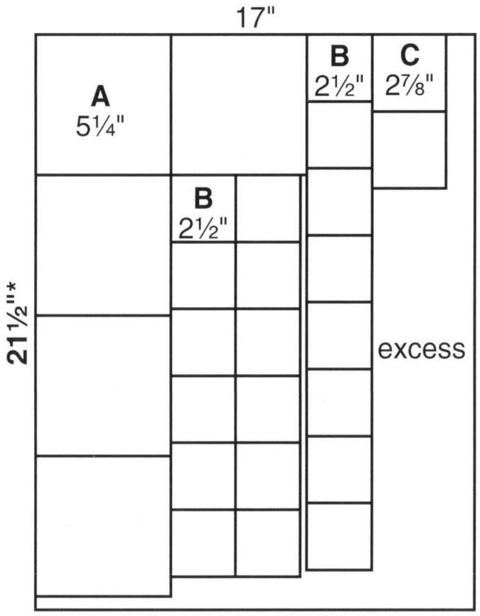

*These light fat quarters must be 21½"

Fig. 2–91. Cutting for light star background (four fat quarters)

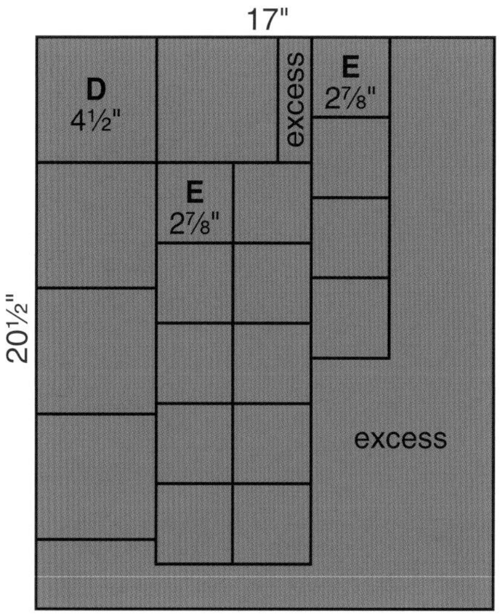

Fig. 2–94. Cutting for dark star centers, star points (one fat quarter)

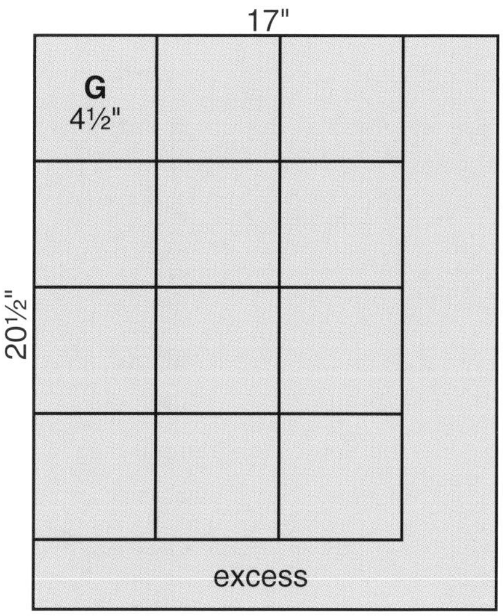

Fig. 2–95. Cutting for stack #1 (four zigzag fat quarters)

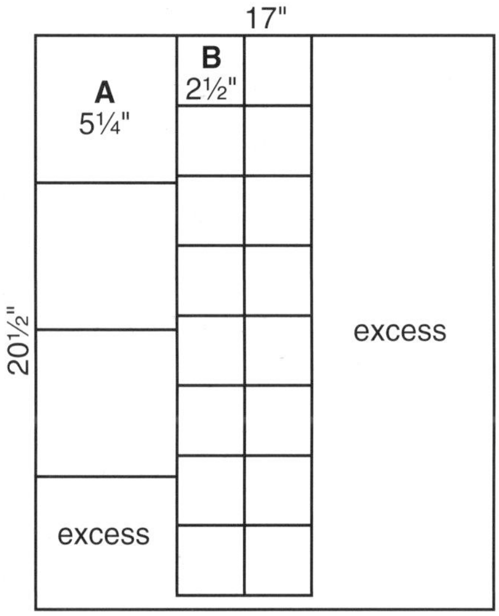

Fig. 2–92. Cutting for light star-background (one fat quarter)

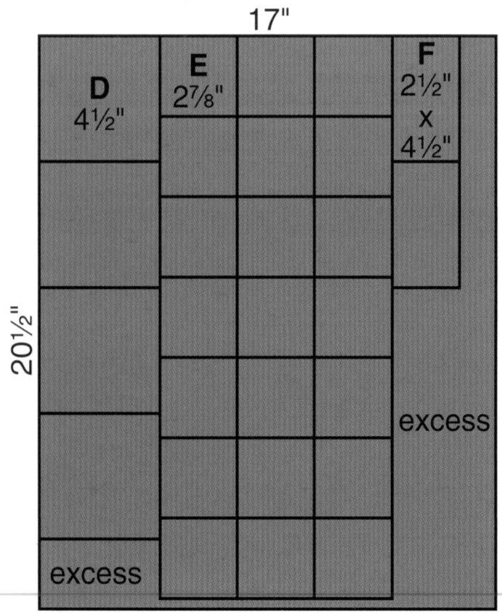

Fig. 2–93. Cutting for dark star centers, star points, half-stars (four fat quarters)

Cutting

Fabric	Patches	Size
4 light star-background fat quarters	5 A squares	5¼"
(fig. 2–91)	20 B squares	2½"
	2 C squares	2⅞"
1 light star-background fat quarter	3 A squares	5¼"
(fig. 2–92)		
	16 B squares	2½"
4 dark fat quarters	4 D squares (star centers)	4½"
(fig. 2–93)	21 E squares (star points)	2⅞"
	2 F rectangles (half-stars)	2½" x 4½"
1 dark fat quarter	5 D squares (star centers)	4½"
(fig. 2–94)	14 E squares (star points)	2⅞"
Stack #1 (four zigzag fat quarters)	12 G squares	4½"
(fig. 2–95)		
Stack #2 (four zigzag fat quarters)	6 H squares*	6⅞"
(fig. 2–96)	*Cut H squares in quarters diagonally.	
Borders & Binding		
Inner border	7 strips 1¼" x 42"	
Outer border	7 strips 4½" x 42"	
Binding	8 strips 2¼" x 42"	

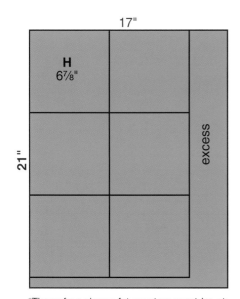

17"

H
6⅞"

21"

excess

*These four zigzag fat quarters must be at least 21" long or you will need two more medium/medium dark fat quarters.

Fig. 2–96. Cutting for stack #2 (four zigzag fat quarters)

before (fig. 2–98). Repeat to make 92 units. You will use 90 of the flying-geese units in the quilt. These units should measure 2½" x 4½".

3. Arrange flying-geese units, D squares, and B squares to make 21 star blocks (fig. 2–99). Use the same star fabric for each star. Each block should measure 8½" square. You will have eight flying-geese units left to use in the half-stars.

4. To make half-square triangle units, mark a diagonal line on the wrong side of six C squares. Layer the marked squares and six E squares right sides together. Sew ¼" on each side of the line. Cut along the line and press the seam allowances toward the star fabric (fig. 2–100). Trim to 2½" square. Make 12.

5. Referring to figure 2–101, make six half-star blocks. For each

block, you will use one flying-geese unit, one F in the same fabric as the star points, two half-square triangles, and two B squares. The blocks should measure 4½" x 8½".

6. To make the 42 zigzag units, use the G squares and H triangles. Select the fabrics at random. Also sew four right zigzag units and two left zigzag units (fig. 2–102).

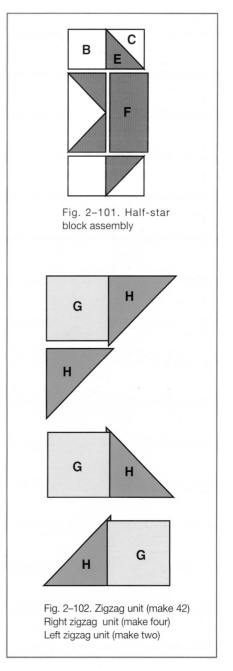

Fig. 2–101. Half-star block assembly

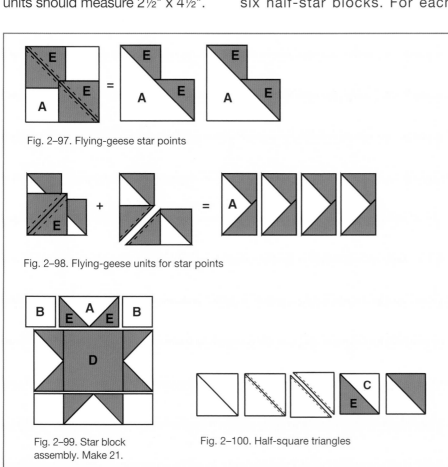

Fig. 2–97. Flying-geese star points

Fig. 2–98. Flying-geese units for star points

Fig. 2–99. Star block assembly. Make 21.

Fig. 2–100. Half-square triangles

Fig. 2–102. Zigzag unit (make 42)
Right zigzag unit (make four)
Left zigzag unit (make two)

Arrange and sew 13 star/zigzag units (fig. 2–103).

7. Referring to figure 2–104, sew the star/zigzag units, the half-star blocks, zigzag units, and triangles into diagonal rows. Then sew the rows together.

8. Join the 1¼" inner border strips to make one continuous strip. Measure the length of the quilt top and cut two pieces from the strip that length. Sew these inner border pieces to the sides of the quilt. Press the seam allowances toward the border. Repeat to make the top and bottom inner border. Repeat with the 4½" outer border strips.

9. Mark your quilting design on the quilt top. We quilted a simple four-petal design in the center of each star and a continuous leaf design in the zigzags and in the outer border.

10. Layer the quilt with backing and batting and quilt by hand or by machine. Sew the 2¼" strips together to make the binding. Bind the quilt, using your favorite method.

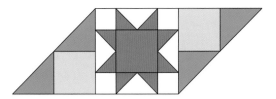

Fig. 2–103. Star/zigzag units. Make 13.

Fig. 2–104. Quilt assembly

Spring Trellis

Quilt size 80" x 80"
SPRING TRELLIS, by Daphne Greig

Gather some wonderful floral prints to make this garden-inspired quilt. Select contrasting light and dark fabrics for the trellis.

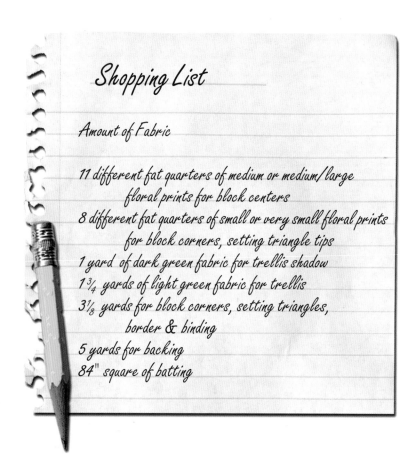

Shopping List

Amount of Fabric

11 different fat quarters of medium or medium/large
floral prints for block centers
8 different fat quarters of small or very small floral prints
for block corners, setting triangle tips
1 yard of dark green fabric for trellis shadow
1 ¾ yards of light green fabric for trellis
3 ⅛ yards for block corners, setting triangles,
border & binding
5 yards for backing
84" square of batting

Cutting Instructions

■ Block Centers
From each of 10 fat quarters, cut four A squares 8½" (fig. 2–105).

From 1 fat quarter, cut one square 8½". You will have a total of 41 A squares.

■ Block Corners,
   Setting Triangle Tips
From each of 8 fat quarters, cut 20 B squares 3½" (fig. 2–106). You will have a total of 160 B squares. Mark a diagonal line on the wrong side of each B square.

■ Trellis Shadows
Cut across the fabric to make 27 strips 1" x 42". From these strips, cut 41 segments 1" x 8½", 41 segments 1" x 9", and 18 segments 1" x 12".

■ Trellis
Cut across the fabric to make 28 strips 2" by 42". From these strips, cut 100 segments 2" x 9" and 60 squares 2".

■ Block Corners
Cut across the fabric to make two strips 3¾" x 42". From these strips, cut 20 C squares 3¾" for the block corners. Mark a diagonal line on the wrong side of each square.

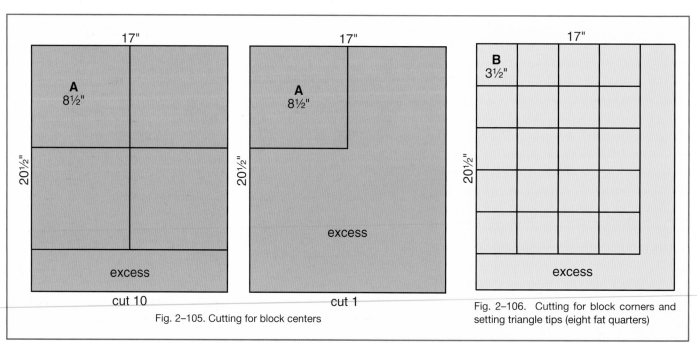

Fig. 2–105. Cutting for block centers

Fig. 2–106. Cutting for block corners and setting triangle tips (eight fat quarters)

■ Side Setting Triangles
Cut two strips 17". Cut the strips into four squares 17". Cut each square in quarters diagonally for a total of 16 triangles (fig. 2–107).

■ Corner Setting Triangles
Cut one strip 10½". From the strip cut two squares 10½". Cut each square in half for a total of four triangles (fig. 2–108).

■ Border & Binding
Cut across the fabric to make eight strips 3½" for the outer border and nine strips 2¼" for the binding.

Sewing the Quilt

1. Use the corner-square method to make the floral print blocks: Place a B square on the corner of an A square, right sides together. Sew on the marked line. Trim the seam allowances to ¼", removing the excess fabric. Press toward the outside (fig. 2–109). Repeat for the other three corners. Make 25 blocks measuring 8½" square (fig. 2–110).

2. Use the same corner technique to make 12 edge blocks with three B corner triangles and one C corner triangle. Note that the border fabric C corner is larger than the other three corners. The blocks should measure 8½" square (fig. 2–111).

3. Use the same corner technique to make four blocks with two B corners and two C corners. The blocks should measure 8½" square (fig. 2–112).

4. Referring to figure 2–113, sew 1" x 8½" and 1" x 9" trellis shadow segments to each center block. Press the seam allowances toward the segments. You will have 25 blocks, measuring 9" square.

5. Referring to figure 2–114, sew 1" x 8½" and 1" x 9" shadow segments to each edge block as shown. Press the seam allowances toward the segments. You will have 12 edge blocks (three of each type) measuring 9" square.

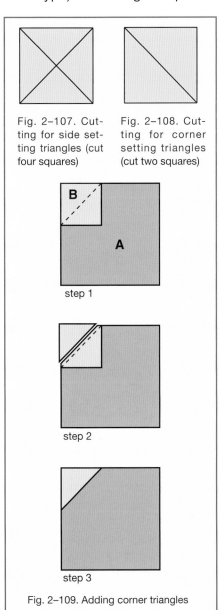

Fig. 2–107. Cutting for side setting triangles (cut four squares)

Fig. 2–108. Cutting for corner setting triangles (cut two squares)

step 1

step 2

step 3

Fig. 2–109. Adding corner triangles

Fig. 2–110. Center blocks (make 25)

Fig. 2–111. Edge blocks (make 12)

Fig. 2–112. Corner blocks (make 4)

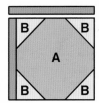

Fig. 2–113. Center blocks with shadow strips (make 25)

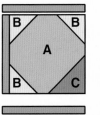

Fig. 2–114. Edge blocks with trellis shadows (make three of each)

6. Referring to figure 2–115, sew 1" x 8½" and 1" x 9" shadow segments to each corner block so that the C triangles are in a different location for each block. Press the seam allowances toward the segments. You will have four blocks (one of each type) measuring 9" square.

7. To make the side setting triangles, place a B square on the corner of a side setting triangle, right sides together. Sew on the marked line. Trim the seam allowance to ¼", removing the excess fabric. Press the seam allowances toward the outside (fig. 2–116). Repeat to make 16 setting triangles.

8. Referring to figure 2–117, sew 1" x 12" dark green shadow segments to 12 of the setting triangles as shown. Four setting triangles have no dark green shadow segments. You will have six 1" x 12" strips of dark green remaining.

9. For the trellis, sew light green 2" squares to light green 2" x 9" strips as shown in figure 2–118. Make two of each length.

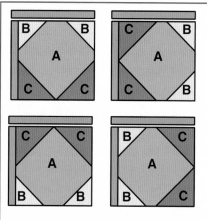

Fig. 2–115. Corner blocks with trellis shadows (Make one of each.)

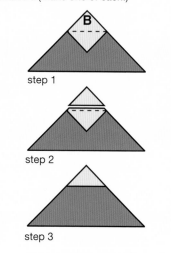

step 1

step 2

step 3

Fig. 2–116. Setting triangles. Make 16.

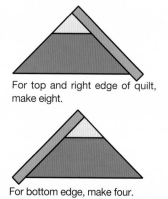

For top and right edge of quilt, make eight.

For bottom edge, make four.

Fig. 2–117. Setting triangles with shadow segments

10. Arrange the blocks, light green trellis strips, remaining dark green shadow strips, and setting triangles in diagonal rows, as shown in figure 2–119, the full quilt diagram.

11. Join the blocks and side setting triangles together for rows 1 through 5, but do not add the corner triangles at this time. Join the first five rows to make one-half of the quilt.

12. For the second half, sew the blocks and remaining shadow segments into rows, but do not add any of the setting triangles yet except for row 9.

13. Sew row 8 to row 9 then add the row 8 setting triangles (fig. 2–120). Continue sewing rows 7 and 6 to the previous rows, adding the side setting triangles after each row has been sewn to the previous one.

14. Join the two halves of the quilt then add the corner setting triangles. Trim the outer edges of the quilt top even, allowing ¾" beyond the corners of the trellis and trellis shadow.

15. Sew the 3½" border strips together in pairs with 45-degree

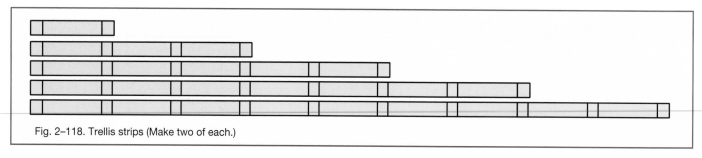

Fig. 2–118. Trellis strips (Make two of each.)

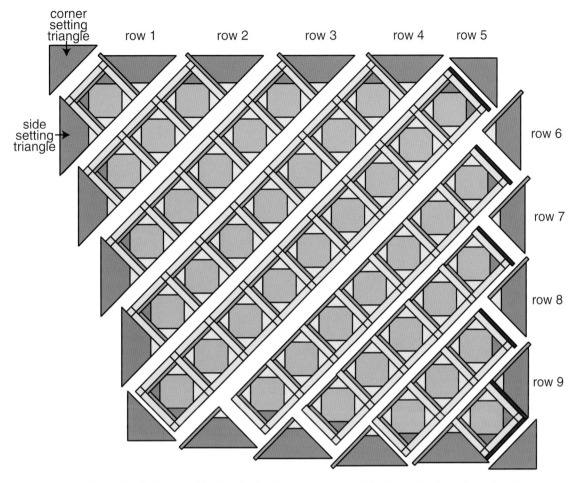

corner setting triangle

row 1   row 2   row 3   row 4   row 5

side setting triangle

row 6

row 7

row 8

row 9

Fig. 2–119. Quilt Assembly. The six shadow segments remaining from step 8 are shown in a darker green.

seams to make four border strips. Sew the border strips to the quilt edges with either butted or mitered corners.

16. Mark your quilting design on the quilt top. We quilted in the ditch around the trellis and trellis shadow and used a continuous flower and leaf design in each block and the border. Layer the quilt top with backing and batting. Quilt by hand or machine. Use the 2¼" strips to bind your quilt.

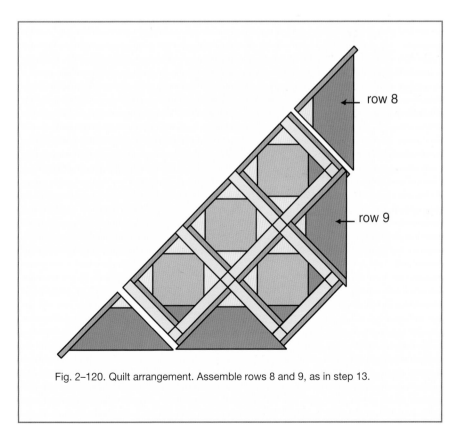

row 8

row 9

Fig. 2–120. Quilt arrangement. Assemble rows 8 and 9, as in step 13.

Family Tree

Quilt size 40" x 40"
FAMILY TREE, by Daphne Greig

Record your family members' names on this fun wall quilt. We used muted reproduction fabrics to give the quilt an old-fashioned feel. Pastel fabrics would be equally nice in this design.

Cutting Instructions

■ **Very Light (block background)**
From one fat quarter, cut 16 A squares 2⅞", and mark a diagonal line on the wrong side of each square. Cut two B squares 6", and cut each square in quarters diagonally. Cut four C squares 2½" (fig. 2–121).

■ **Light**
From one fat quarter, cut 12 A squares 2⅞", and mark a diagonal line on the wrong side of each square. Cut four C squares 2½" (fig. 2–122).

■ **Red Print & Green Print**
From each fat quarter, cut 14 A squares 2⅞" (fig. 2–123).

■ **Dark Green**
From one fat quarter, cut two squares 6⅞", and cut each square in half for four D triangles. Cut four inner border strips 2" x 17" (fig. 2–124, page 78).

Shopping List

Amount of Fabric

1 very light fat quarter for block background
1 light print fat quarter for trees
1 red print fat quarter for trees
1 green print fat quarter for trees
1 dark green fat quarter for trees & inner border
1 brown fat quarter tree trunks & inner border
3 different gold fat quarters for center square and setting triangles
1 burgundy fat quarter for sashing
¾ yard for outer border & binding
1⅜ yards for backing
44" square of batting

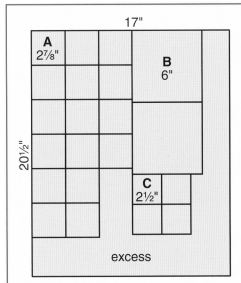

Fig. 2–121. Cutting for very light background fabric (one fat quarter)

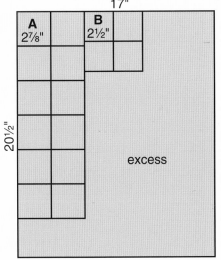

Fig. 2–122. Cutting for light fabric (one fat quarter)

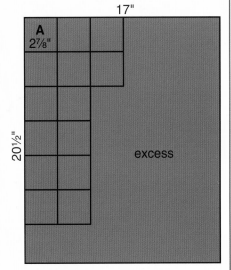

Fig. 2–123. Cutting for red print and green print (one fat quarter of each color)

■ **Brown**

From one fat quarter, cut four E rectangles 2¼" x 5". Cut four F squares 2½", and mark a diagonal line on the wrong side of each square. Cut four inner border strips 2" x 17" (fig. 2–125).

■ **Gold**

From one fat quarter, cut one square 10½" for the center of the quilt and four squares 2" for the cornerstones.

From one fat quarter, cut one square 15½". Cut the square in quarters diagonally for four side setting triangles (fig. 2–126).

From one fat quarter, cut two squares 8". Cut each square in half diagonally for four corner setting triangles (fig. 2–127).

■ **Burgundy**

From one fat quarter, cut 16 sashes 1½" x 10½" and 12 cornerstones 1½" (fig. 2–128).

■ **Outer Border & Binding**

Cut across the fabric to make four strips 3½" for the outer border. Cut four strips 2¼" for binding.

Sewing the Quilt

1. Layer eight very light A squares and eight green print A squares, right sides together. Sew ¼" on each side of the marked line. Cut along the line and press the seam allowances toward the green print. Trim to 2½" square (fig. 2–129). You will have 16 half-square-triangle leaf units.

2. Repeat with the remaining A squares, as follows: eight very light and eight red print squares, six light print and six green print squares, and six light print and six red print squares.

3. Sew one very light B triangle to each side of a brown E rectangle to make a tree trunk. Press the seam allowances toward the

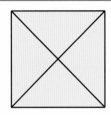

Fig. 2–126. Cut one 15½" square for side setting triangles.

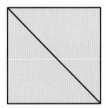

Fig. 2–127. Cut one 8" square for corner setting triangles.

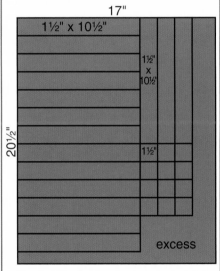

Fig. 2–128. Cutting for burgundy fabric (one fat quarter)

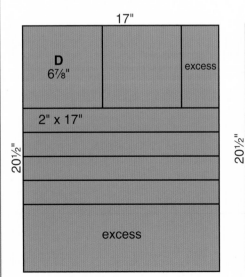

Fig. 2–124. Cutting for dark green fabric (one fat quarter)

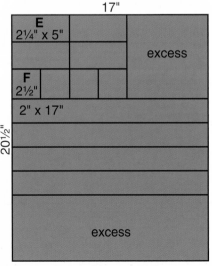

Fig. 2–125. Cutting for brown fabric (one fat quarter)

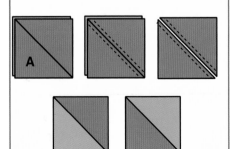

Fig. 2–129. Leaf units (make 16)

trunk. Trim the end of the brown rectangle even with the triangles (fig. 2–130).

4. Place one brown F square over the bottom corner, right sides together. Sew on the marked line. Trim the seam allowances to ¼", removing the excess fabric. Press the seam allowances toward the outside (fig. 2–131). Make four tree trunk units.

5. Referring to figure 2–132, make four tree blocks. The leaf units can be distributed randomly among the four blocks. Each block should measure 10½" square.

6. Referring to the quilt assembly diagram (fig. 2–133 on page 80), join the tree blocks, burgundy sashing strips and squares, center square, and setting triangles. Trim the sashing squares on the outer edge, even with the setting triangles, to straighten the outer edges.

7. For the inner border, sew pairs of dark green strips together to make two long strips. Press the seam allowances open. Repeat with the brown strips.

8. Measure the width and length of the quilt. Trim the dark green strips to match the length and the brown strips to match the width. Referring to the quilt assembly diagram, sew the inner border strips and cornerstones to the quilt top, pressing seam allowances toward the border strips.

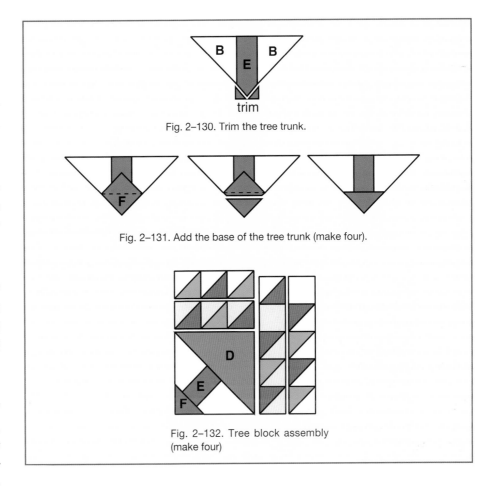
Fig. 2–130. Trim the tree trunk.

Fig. 2–131. Add the base of the tree trunk (make four).

Fig. 2–132. Tree block assembly (make four)

9. Measure the length of the quilt and cut two outer border strips to match. Sew to the sides of the quilt. Press the seam allowances toward the borders.

10. Measure the width of the quilt, including the outer borders, and cut two strips that length. Sew them to the top and the bottom of the quilt top. Press the seam allowances toward the borders.

11. If you like, you can embroider your last name and the names of your family members in the center square and setting triangles. (Write the names with

a fabric marker that can be removed.) Use three strands of embroidery floss and stem stitch for the embroidery (fig. 2–134).

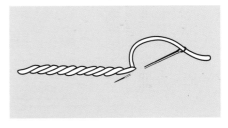
Fig. 2–134. Stem stitch. Each stitch goes to the right half of the stitch length, then comes back to the left, the needle emerging below the end of the stitch made earlier.

12. Mark your quilting design on the quilt. We quilted around the patches of the tree blocks and

¼" inside the sashing strips and inner borders. We used feather designs for the center square and setting triangles. A cable design completes the outer border.

13. Layer the quilt with backing and batting and then quilt by hand or by machine. Make the binding with the 2½" strips. Bind the quilt, using your favorite method.

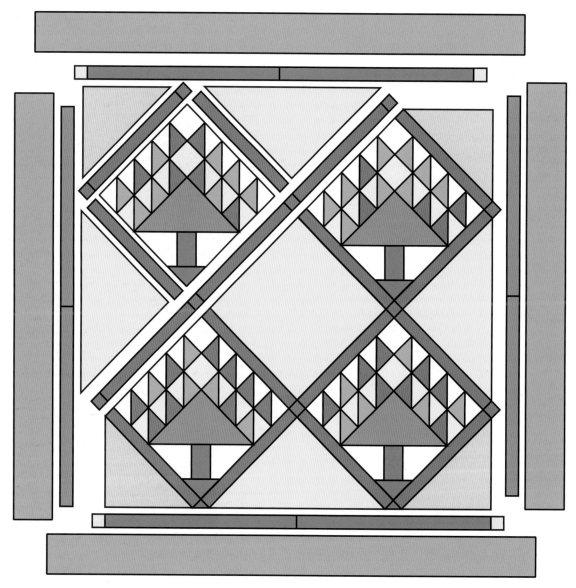

Fig. 2–133. Quilt assembly

Victory Star

Quilt size 46" x 46"
VICTORY STAR, by Susan Purney-Mark

This complex-looking quilt is made with easy half-square triangles and fast flying geese. The open areas between the blocks provide a lot of opportunity for detailed quilting designs. There are many possible color and fabric combinations you could try ... maybe bright crayon colors on a black background?

Shopping List

Amount of Fabric

8 different fat quarters* of light fabric
    for background & inner border
5 different fat quarters of red fabric
    for stars & outer borders
½ yard for binding
3 yards for backing
50" square of batting

*The eight light fat quarters need to be at least 21" long, or you
will need two extra fat quarters to cut the 1½" x 17" strips.

line, corner to corner, on the wrong side of 24 red A squares. Layer each one on a red A of a different fabric, right sides together. Sew ¼" on each side of the line. Cut along the line and press the seam allowances open. Trim to measure 2½" square (fig. 2–137). You will use these in step 8.

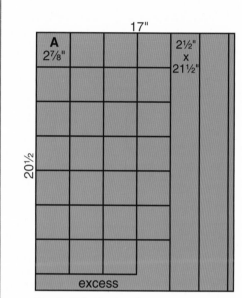

Fig. 2–135. Cutting for stars and outer borders (five fat quarters)

Cutting Instructions

Cut patches from fat quarters, as listed in the following table.

Sewing the Quilt

1. To make half-square triangle units, mark a diagonal

Cutting

Fabric	Pieces	Size
5 red fat quarters (fig. 2–135)	27 A squares	2⅞"
	2 strips	2½"
8 light fat quarters (fig. 2–136)	2 B squares	6½"
	2 C squares	5¼"
	2 D squares	4⅜"
	2 E squares	3⅜"
	7 F squares	2½"
	3 strips	1½" x 17
Binding	5 strips	2¼" x 42"

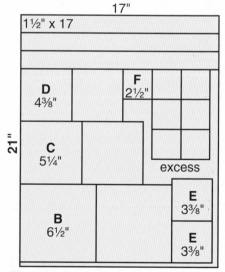

*These light fat quarters must be at least 21" long.

Fig. 2–136. Cutting for background and inner border (eight fat quarters)

2. To make the square-in-a-square units, cut 32 red A squares in half diagonally. Referring to figure 2–138, sew two red A triangles to opposite sides of an E square. Press the seam allowances toward the triangles. Repeat for the remaining corners to complete a unit. Make 16 units measuring 4½" square.

3. For the fast flying geese, mark a diagonal line, corner to corner, on the wrong side of 48 red A squares. Layer two red A squares right sides together with one light C square. Sew ¼" on each side of the line. Cut along

Fig. 2–137. Half-square triangle units (make 48)

the line and press the small triangles away from the large triangle (fig. 2–139). You will have 4 C squares remaining.

4. Layer one red square right sides together with A/C unit, as shown in figure 2–140. Sew ¼" on each side of the marked lines. Cut along the marked line and press the small triangles away from the large triangle. The flying geese units should measure 2½" x 4½". From the remaining 7 red squares, trim 4 to 1½" square to use in step 12 as cornerstones.

5. For the corner units, place a D square on one corner of a B square as shown in figure 2–141. (It's more interesting when the large and the small squares are different light fabrics.) Sew along the marked line

and trim away the excess triangle. Press the triangle in place to form the B/D unit, which should measure 6½" square.

6. For each corner unit, use one B/D unit, two flying-geese units, and three light F squares. Referring to figure 2–142, assemble 16 corner units that measure 8½" square. From the remaining 8 light squares, use 4 in step 12 as cornerstones.

7. For each center unit, use one flying-geese unit, two half-square triangles, and one square-in-a-square unit. Referring to figure 2–143, assemble 16 center units measuring 4½" x 8½".

8. Referring to fig. 2–144, make four pinwheel units that measure 4½" square.

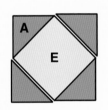   

Fig. 2–138. Square-in-a-square A/E unit (make 16)

Fig. 2–139. The first step for fast flying geese

Fig. 2–140. Flying geese units for star points (make 48)

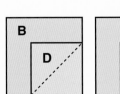 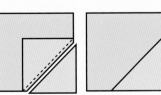 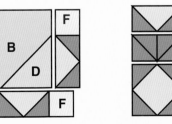

Fig. 2–141. B/D unit (make 16)

Fig. 2–142. Corner unit (make 16)

Fig. 2–143. Center unit (make 16)

Fig. 2–144. Pinwheel unit (make four)

9. Arrange and sew one pin-wheel unit, four corner units, and four center units to form a Victory Star block (fig. 2–145). It should measure 20½" square.

10. Referring to figure 2–146, sew four Victory Stars together. Sew light fabric border strips together with 45-degree seams, alternating the fabrics. Join red border strips in the same way.

11. Measure the length and width of the quilt and cut four light border strips to that length. Sew border strips to two sides of the quilt. Press the seam allowances toward the border.

12. Add the red cornerstones to each end of the remaining light strips. Sew these strips to the top and bottom of the quilt. Repeat with the red border strips and light cornerstones to make the outer borders (fig. 2–146).

13. Mark your quilting design on the quilt top. We quilted an intricate floral design in the light areas and ¼" inside the star blocks. The borders were quilted in a small cable design. Layer the quilt with backing and batting and then quilt by hand or by machine.

14. Sew the 2¼" strips together to make the binding. Bind the quilt, using your favorite method.

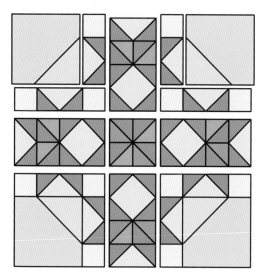

Fig. 2–145. Victory Star assembly (make four)

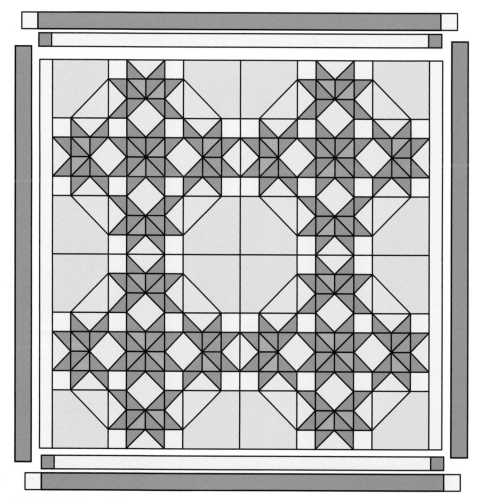

Fig. 2–146. Quilt assembly

Lesson Plans
for teachers

Teachers are welcome to use this book to develop classes from its many projects. You will have fun introducing the versatility of fat quarters to your students. The book is written with the assumption that the student has completed at least one quilt and has basic quilting skills, such as rotary cutting and chain and machine piecing.

We have suggested a class length with each project, but you will need to adapt it to suit you, your shop, and your students. We are assuming one session equals three hours. Sometimes it is more fun to put the sessions together and make a full-day class. You may also choose to have the students do the precutting before class to allow them to get right into the fun stuff! Just make sure they know how to use the cutting diagrams with each project.

The lesson plans for each chapter also include any special requirements for your classroom and the particular skills you can teach in each project.

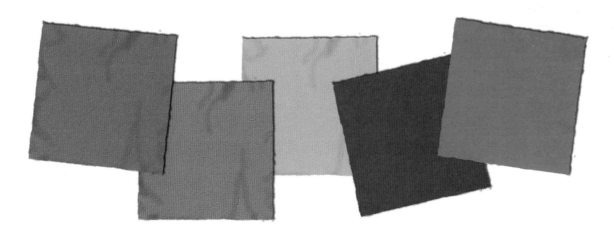

FOUR PATCH HARMONY

Number of sessions	2 (could be a full day if fabric is precut)
Classroom requirements	Design walls for each student in session 2
Skills emphasis	Good rotary-cutting skills, color play with fabrics

Outline

In session one, show students the importance of choosing and arranging fabrics by using a color wheel and playing with value and contrast. This is a good class for flannel or theme quilts because the shapes are large and basic. Students could come to session one with their fabrics all precut and could begin sewing right away.

In the second session, students bring their completed blocks and use a design wall to play with possible layouts. Show students how to use a reducing lens or binoculars to pick out areas that need work. Discuss finishing techniques, including the quilting choices and layering, quilting, and binding.

LOLLY HEARTS

Number of sessions	2
Classroom requirements	Appliqué pressing sheets
Skills emphasis	Appliqué methods

Outline

This class is great for an introduction to using fusible web products. Discuss the different fusibles and the variety of threads for machine appliqué.

In the first session, students cut their fat quarters and put the top together. In the second session, students complete their appliqué units, fuse them in place and sandwich the layers together. Encourage students to make a test sandwich to try the different settings and stitches on their machines for the appliqué. Once the appliqué is completed, discuss possible quilting options for the background and options for binding the quilt.

MOON RINGS

Number of sessions	2
Classroom requirements	Design walls for each student in session 2
Skills emphasis	Half-square triangles, appliqué methods

Outline

Teach several appliqué techniques in this class. In session one, demonstrate several hand and machine techniques. Have students try each method and select the one they prefer for their quilt. Have students make their blocks during this session and at home before session two.

In the second class, show students how to square their blocks then show them several quilt layouts. Students use the design walls to try different arrangements then sew their blocks together. Discuss finishing, including quilting choices and layering, quilting, and binding.

BAMBOO GROVE

Number of sessions	1 for table runner
	2 for wall quilt
Classroom requirements	Design walls for each student for wall quilt
Skills emphasis	Machine appliqué

Outline

One session (table runner):
Demonstrate use of fusible web and accurate positioning for leaves. Show students how to use a narrow zigzag stitch to appliqué leaves to the background squares. Discuss thread options for this step. Help students arrange and sew rows of leaves. Demonstrate measuring rows to cut accurate sashing strip and borders. Discuss simple method to layer, sew, and turn the table runner. Discuss quilting choices.

Two sessions (wall quilt):
Demonstrate use of fusible web and making blocks in one session. Have students make 66 leaf blocks before session two. In session two, students arrange their blocks on design walls. They can rotate the blocks for different arrangements. Discuss accurate measuring and cutting for lengthwise strips and borders. Discuss quilt finishing, including layering, quilting, and binding.

DANCING STARS

Number of sessions	2 (could be a full day if fabric is precut)
Classroom requirements	Design walls for each student in session 2
Skills emphasis	A "relaxed" piecing method

Outline

Demonstrate the piecing method to students. Explain how placement of squares is flexible and results can vary. We recommend that you have several "in progress" blocks made to illustrate how varying the placement of the squares makes different blocks. Stress the importance of paying attention to the two piecing sequences. You may recommend to the students that they keep their two fabric groups separate. Show students the variety of skinny to fat stars that are possible. Make certain they understand the two piecing sequences before they leave. Students should complete the required number of blocks as homework.

In session two, students use the design wall to lay out their blocks, paying attention to repeating fabrics and correct placement of the two kinds of blocks. Discuss layering, quilting, and binding.

GREEN TEA

Number of sessions	2 (could be a full day if fabric is precut)
Classroom requirements	Design walls for each student in session 2
Skills emphasis	Half-square triangles

Outline

Demonstrate making accurate half-square triangles, following the instructions on pages 38–39. Stress the importance of trimming accurately. Demonstrate block arrangement and have students make a total of 16 blocks before session two. Help students arrange and sew blocks, spacers and sashing strips in session two. Discuss layering, quilting, and binding. Be sure to stress the importance of even quilting to maintain a flat quilt.

WOVEN SQUARES TABLE RUNNER

Number of sessions   1 (2 sessions if only two hours each)
Skills emphasis   Setting triangles, color options (seasonal, monochromatic)

Outline

Demonstrate the importance of keeping cut pieces separated into blocks and making all of one block before proceeding to the next. This avoids confusion. Other design options are possible by placing the blocks in different sequences or rotating them. Show this to the students before they assemble the blocks and triangles into the runner. This runner provides a great way to use seasonal fabrics or to match their décor. It also makes a nice gift.

EMPRESS TILES

Number of sessions   2 (could be full day if fabric is cut into 4½" strips)
Classroom requirements   Design walls for block layout
Skills emphasis   Color play, relaxed cutting method, alternate layouts

Outline

In session one, demonstrate stacking, cutting, and sequencing for the strips. Make sure students understand the importance of keeping the cut triangles in sewing sequence. Demonstrate the sewing of one strip unit, pressing the seam allowances in one direction, and trimming the strip to 12½".

Session two can be devoted to showing students that they can play with different arrangements for placing the strips in the blocks, then placing the blocks in the quilt layout. We recommend you have several strip units and blocks ready for demonstrating this on the design wall.

This fat quarter project can also be used if students want to exchange cut strips to add more fabric variety to their blocks. They can also exchange sewn strip units. Spend time discussing quilting options. Suggest that machine quilting would be the best choice because of the multiple seams. Discuss finishing techniques.

LAYERED PINWHEELS

Number of sessions	2
Skills emphasis	Making and using templates, selecting color values for blocks, block pressing to ensure accuracy

Outline

Demonstrate and have students make templates A and B. Be sure they include the grain line on each template. Discuss different color values for the blocks. Demonstrate cutting accurate shapes. Show students how to sew one layered pinwheel block and stress accuracy. Refer them to the pressing plan shown on page 50. Have students make 35 blocks before session two. During session two, discuss block arrangement and quilt assembly, including the addition of borders. Discuss quilting options and quilt finishing techniques.

MANY RISING STARS

Number of sessions	2
Skills emphasis	Good rotary-cutting skills, selecting color values for block backgrounds, quick piecing for star points

Outline

Students cut and sort their fabrics as described in the cutting instructions. Be sure to emphasize accurate cutting and strong value contrast for light and dark fat quarters for block backgrounds. Demonstrate the sewing method for quick star points and have students make the inner sawtooth stars before the next session. In session two, show students how to arrange their fabrics for adding the middle and outer star points. Stress accuracy with each step so the blocks will measure correctly. Discuss block arrangement, quilt assembly, quilting options, and quilt finishing techniques.

SNAILS IN MY GARDEN

Number of sessions	2
Skills emphasis	Appliqué methods, including three-dimensional appliqué

Outline

Students can precut for the Snail's Trail and Flower blocks. In the first class, demonstrate piecing the Snail's Trail blocks. Pay particular attention to the arrangement of colors for these blocks. Demonstrate Flower block backgrounds and have students finish these and the Snail's Trail blocks for the next class.

In session two, show students how to appliqué the leaves to the Flower block. You can show hand and machine appliqué and have students select the method they want to use. Also show how to make the three-dimensional flower petals and the flower centers. Discuss color arrangement, borders, and quilt finishing.

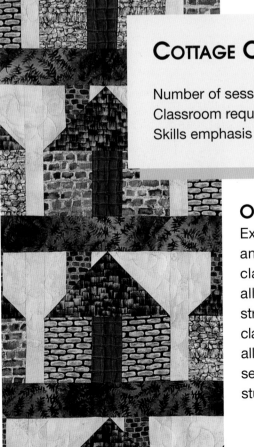

COTTAGE COUNTRY

Number of sessions	2
Classroom requirements	Design walls for each student in session 2
Skills emphasis	Quick strip piecing, horizontal strip quilt layout

Outline

Experienced students can select and precut their fabrics for this class. Stress accurate ¼" seam allowances for sewing. Demonstrate the house blocks in the first class and have students complete all their house blocks before the second class. In the second class, students will find it helpful to use a

design wall to arrange their house blocks. Show students how to measure their horizontal rows and cut sky and grass strips to match. This will ensure a flat, even quilt top. Discuss borders and quilt finishing. This is a good time to recommend a machine quilting workshop for students.

ZIGZAG STARS

Number of sessions	2
Classroom requirements	Design walls for each student in session 2
Skills emphasis	Half-square triangles, quick piecing for star points, diagonal quilt layout

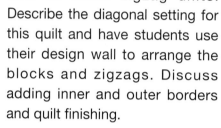

Outline

Students can precut their fat quarters before coming to class. During session one, demonstrate Sawtooth Star blocks and have students make blocks during class and at home. Also demonstrate half star blocks and ask students to complete these as well.

In session two, show students how to make zigzag units. Describe the diagonal setting for this quilt and have students use their design wall to arrange the blocks and zigzags. Discuss adding inner and outer borders and quilt finishing.

SPRING TRELLIS

Number of sessions	2
Classroom requirements	Design walls for each student in session 2
Skills emphasis	Quick piecing techniques, on-point quilt setting

Outline

Students can precut their fabrics before class. In the first session, show students how to sew the three different blocks that are needed for the quilt. Then show students how to add trellis shadow strips to their blocks. Stress the importance of following the piecing diagrams to make the correct type and number of blocks. Have students complete all these blocks before session two. Students can use a design wall to arrange their blocks before sewing. Because this is a large quilt, students may want to work on the arrangement at home and label the arrangement to bring back to the second class.

In session two, show students how to prepare their setting triangles and trellis strips. Carefully explain the quilt layout and sewing method. Pay particular attention to the sewing instructions for the bottom right rows of the quilt. Students may need extra space when laying out and sewing their quilts. Demonstrate the addition of the outer border and discuss quilting and finishing techniques.

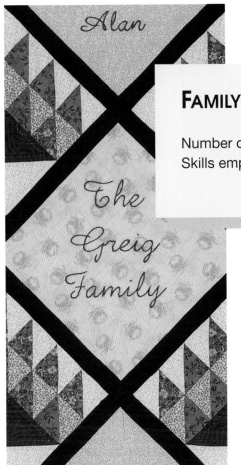

FAMILY TREE

Number of sessions   2
Skills emphasis   Half-square triangles, on-point setting, stem-stitch embroidery

Outline

Students can precut their fabrics for this class. During session one, show students how to make half-square triangles and how to make the Tree blocks. Be sure students arrange their half-square triangles in a random way among the blocks.

Discuss the on-point quilt layout and borders in session two and have students make the quilt top. Demonstrate using the stem stitch to embroider names in the center square and setting triangles. Discuss quilting designs and quilt finishing techniques.

VICTORY STAR

Number of sessions   2 or 3
Skills emphasis   Half-square triangles, fast flying geese, square-in-a-square

Outline

During session one, demonstrate half-square triangles. You may want to introduce students to the variety of paper products that can be used to produce accurate half-square triangles. Demonstrate the fast flying geese method. Demonstrate

square-in-a-square units. In session two, show students the importance of the joining sequence for each unit. Discuss border options, if desired. Discuss quilting options for background areas, and finishing techniques.

Suggestions for Additional Classes:

Machine Quilting Class – Teach students both straight-line and free-motion quilting techniques. An advanced session can include use of specialty threads.

Hand Quilting Class – Teach students about needles, thread, thimbles, quilt marking, and the quilting stitch.

Quilt Finishing Workshop – Have students create a practice quilt top, and show binding methods and application of sleeves and labels.

Resources

Susan and Daphne are available for teaching and lecturing engagements.

Patchworks Studio
Susan Purney-Mark and Daphne Greig, co-owners
2552 Eastdowne Road
Victoria, BC V8R 5P9
Canada

Telephone: 250-595-4411
Fax: 250-595-4377

Email: patchworkstudio@shaw.ca
www.patchworkstudio.com

Starr Designs Hand Dyed Fabrics
P.O. Box 440
1300 S. Hwy 3
Etna, CA 96027

Telephone: 530-467-5121
Fax: 530-467-5160

E-mail info@starrfabrics.com
www.starrfabrics.com

Daphne Greig began quilting in 1984 when she enrolled in a beginner class at a local shop. She jumped in with both feet to cover all the beds and many walls with quilts and now refers to her life before this time as "BQ" — Before Quilting!

Daphne has had several careers including secretary, financial coordinator, and data analyst, but her career as a quilt designer, teacher, and author is the most fun and rewarding. She is an enthusiastic and patient teacher, encouraging her students to try new techniques and expand their repertoire of skills.

Together with Susan Purney-Mark, she has developed a successful pattern company, Patchworks Studio. They have designed, published, and marketed over 50 quilt patterns and co-authored *Quilted Havens - City Houses, Country Homes*, published by the American Quilter's Society.

Daphne regularly writes articles for several quilting magazines and teaches internationally and online at Quilt University. Her work has been exhibited in Canada and the United States. Daphne lives with her husband, Alan, in North Saanich, a rural community near Victoria, British Columbia.

Susan began quilting in 1977 and continues to learn by creating and designing. Her interest in quilting techniques, history, fiber, and design has supplied her with inspiration to last a lifetime and more. She shares her enthusiasm and skills with others through teaching, traveling, and writing.

Susan has studied and taught in Canada, the United States, and overseas. In 1996, she formed a quilt pattern company, Patchworks Studio, www.patchworkstudio.com, with Daphne Greig. Together they have created more than 50 unique designs, including a quick reverse appliqué technique for stained-glass quilts. They also collaborated on their first book, *Quilted Havens*, published by AQS in 2000. In addition, Susan is on the faculty of Quilt University, www.quiltuniversity.com.

Other AQS Books

This is only a small selection of the books available from the American Quilter's Society. AQS books are known worldwide for timely topics, clear writing, beautiful color photos, and accurate illustrations and patterns. The following books are available from your local bookseller, quilt shop, or public library.

#6511   us$22.95

#4995   us$19.95

#6295   us$24.95

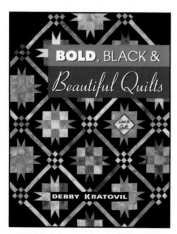

#6515   us$19.95

#5336   us$22.95

#5755   us$21.95

#5850   us$21.95

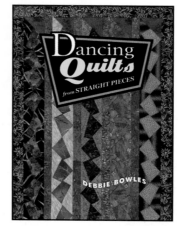

#6210   us$24.95

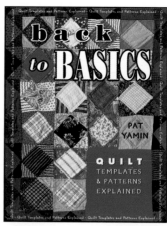

#6293   us$24.95

LOOK for these books nationally. CALL 1-800-626-5420 or VISIT our Web site at www.AmericanQuilter.com